SECRET OF THE THIRD SIDE OF THE COIN

Secret of the Third Side of the Coin
By **Sirshree** Tejparkhi

Copyright © Tejgyan Global Foundation

All Rights Reserved 2017

Tejgyan Global Foundation is a charitable organization
with its headquarters in Pune, India.

ISBN : 978-81-8415-640-9

Published by WOW Publishings Pvt. Ltd., India

First edition published in July 2017

Fifth reprint in February 2025

Printed and bound by Trinity Academy For Corporate Training Ltd, Pune

Copyright and publishing rights are vested exclusively with WOW Publishings Pvt. Ltd. This book is sold subject to the condition that it shall not by way of trade or otherwise, be lent, resold, hired out, or otherwise circulated without the publisher's prior written consent in any form of binding or cover other than that in which it is published and without a similar condition including this condition being imposed on the subsequent purchaser and without limiting the rights under copyright reserved above, no part of this publication may be reproduced, stored in or introduced into a retrieval system, or transmitted, in any form, or by any means, electronic, mechanical, photocopying, recording or otherwise, without the prior written permission of both the copyright owner and the above-mentioned publisher of this book. Any person who does any unauthorized act in relation to this publication may be liable to criminal prosecution and civil claims for damages.

Although the author and publisher have made every effort to ensure accuracy of content in this book, they hereby disclaim any liability to any party for any loss, damage, or disruption caused by errors or omissions, resulting from negligence, accident, or any other cause. Readers are advised to take full responsibility to exercise discretion in understanding and applying the content of this book.

Preface

We go through a variety of experiences in life. We keep moving from one experience to the next. One moment we feel happy, sad at the next. We experience clarity in one moment and confusion in the next.

These fluctuations between the extremes of life pose a challenge for us. They come with the purpose of leading us deeper into the real truths about life. We may settle for certain answers and try to fix those as our life philosophy. But no sooner does life throw up a new challenge, than we find that those answers, which we have held onto, no longer work for us.

Life abounds in profound and paradoxical secrets that transcend all questions. These secrets defy the limited perspectives from which questions arise. They lead us beyond the dualities of life.

The consideration that there can be a third side of a coin baffles the human intellect. The mind that is used to dwelling in logical confines cannot fathom a third side. Every coin has two sides to it. These two sides represent the extremes in life. However, there is a third side that exists between these two… or rather, beyond these two. It is the fine edge of the coin!

We are quick to choose either "Heads" or "Tails" at the toss of the coin. But the third side of the coin, along the edge, is neither

"Heads" nor "Tails". It is the razor-edge between the two opposing sides. Paradoxically, it holds the two polarities together.

The third side of the coin is the openness with which we approach life without any fixations, without prejudices. When we abide in this state of openness to life as it unfolds, we go beyond the duality of opposites. We are free from the extremes of life. We need to learn to stay on the edge—the third side—without slipping into any of the opposites. We are not holding onto anything, nor are we trying to escape anything. We are just present in the Heart of existence!

Dwelling on the third side, on the edge beyond polarities, we find that we are not in discord with anything in life. We are in harmony with everything that unfolds in the flow of life. Such a life abounds in bliss unspeakable! It has a sense of balance, where nothing can touch our equipoise.

When you find that your mind is trying to hold onto fixed ideas, it is holding onto a particular side of the coin. The mind prefers one side and rejects the other side. It vacillates between attachment and aversion to the polarities of life. Life then is like a pendulum that oscillates between two extremes. The invitation to the third side of the coin is about moving to the base of the pendulum, which never moves.

Discovering the third side of the coin in every aspect of life is an illuminating experience. We don't hold onto any outcomes, we don't fix any answers. We flow with the way life unfolds. We open ourselves to the most wondrous insights. The secrets of life are unraveled to us intuitively.

The secrets that reside on either side of the coin are half-secrets. Many of the so-called secrets that are popular in the world today are actually "half-secrets"! They explain a limited perspective of life. Half-secrets are discovered from a limited standpoint where the full picture of life is not clearly seen.

When one learns to be present on the third side of the coin, you see everything for what it truly is. You see everything in totality. You receive insights, which can be called the full-secrets. There are numerous missing links in the way we see life. These missing links are unraveled only from the third side of the coin of life.

This book expounds the full-secrets of various facets of life. These full-secrets lead us beyond the half-secrets that we have known so far. The missing links that are explained in this book expose the limited viewpoint that shows only the half-secret.

Each chapter in the book discusses a particular topic by explaining the prevalent beliefs and viewpoints and then explaining the full-secret in the light of higher wisdom.

The missing links that are brought to light begin with existential aspects like prayer, desires, and destiny, and then move onto the deeper more profound aspects of spirituality.

It is recommended that you read the chapters in sequence the first time, after which you can zoom in on any particular topic of your choice for reading again.

Wish you an enlightening journey through this book!

Contents

Preface		iii
1.	Bringing Completeness to Prayer	1
2.	Beyond Virtuousness	12
3.	True Love – The Wellspring Within You	22
4.	Living in the Present	35
5.	Dissolving Problems	43
6.	Beyond Personality and Character	52
7.	The Ultimate Goal of Life	61
8.	You are Meditation	71
9.	Desires – To Have or Not to Have	80
10.	The Motivation for Karma	89
11.	The Basis for Result of Karma	99
12.	Whatever Happens is for Growth	110
13.	The Magic of Forgiveness	123
14.	Rebirth and Liberation	136

15.	Spirituality Beyond Occult Practices	145
16.	Self-Experience – Beyond Duality	154
17.	Align with the Divine Will	161
18.	Essence of Spiritual Practice	170
19.	Transcending Knowledge	181
20.	The Twofold Path Leading to One	191

Bibliography   201

1
Bringing Completeness to Prayer

Every religion instills the importance of prayer. Whether you are a Hindu or a Muslim, a Christian or a Sikh, a Parsi, a Jain or a Buddhist, prayer is a foundation principle of every religion. Prayer has such power that anything in the world can be changed and anything you want can be attained. Even doctors treating terminally ill patients ask their family members to resort to prayer as the last option. People have indeed risen to life from the verge of death through the power of prayer.

Everything is available in abundance. Things are waiting to manifest in your life. But the window is closed. Sunlight is waiting for the window to be opened, so that it can enter. Prayer with gratitude is the method of opening that window and allowing the flow of abundance in your life.

Prayer is the means to manifest life. Prayer is not merely what is ritualistically practiced with folded hands and closed eyes. Every thought that receives your attention is a prayer. Prayer is put up to the Source, or the Universe, or the Creative principle. Everything is available to be experienced in life. Prayer leads you to a state of receptivity so that what you are praying for can manifest in your life.

Half-secret
Ask through prayer.

The power of prayer is miraculous. You can achieve anything you aspire for, through the power of prayer. Prayer is constantly functioning in each of our lives at all times, whether we are aware of it or not. When we are aware of how the power of prayer works in our lives, we can give it a direction and harness its power. When we pray for something, we create vibrations in the universe that resonate with what we are praying for.

But this remains only half the secret when you are unaware of what needs to be done after praying. Most people commit one of the following mistakes after praying, resulting in failure of prayer.

1. Imagining

Let us understand this with the help of a parable.

> A massive flood once inundated a village. Everyone feared for their lives and started looking for ways to escape. A devotee of God too lived in that village. He had full faith in God. He started praying, "Dear God, please come and rescue me." Just then, a few people waded across the water with ropes in hand.

They flung a rope towards him and asked him to grab it. But he declined the offer and said, "My God will come and rescue me."

The water was rising. After some time, a few people came towards him in a boat and asked him to hop on. But again he replied, "Thanks, but no; my God will come and rescue me." The water was rapidly rising, so he went atop the roof of his house and continued his prayer to God. A military helicopter then descended upon his house and lowered a ladder for him to climb. But the man again refused to accept the help saying that his God would come and rescue him. The water soon rose above his head and he drowned.

After he died, he complained to God, "You let me down! Why didn't you stand up to my faith and come to rescue me?" God replied, "I did come to your rescue thrice – once with a rope, once in a rescue boat, and once in a helicopter. But you didn't recognize me and refused to take my help."

This man was a victim of his imaginings. This story can be helpful in shedding light on our own imaginings, assumptions and expectations regarding how our prayers should be fulfilled. Man forms several assumptions through what he sees on television, reads in books and hears from various sources like priests, clerics, ascetics, etc. Unless he gets to know the full secret of prayer and what to do after praying, he may fall victim to one of these.

2. Presuming

Sometimes due to our prayers, some incidents happen in life that seem to be negative on the outside. As a result we stop praying.

However, many a time, such incidents that appear to be negative at first turn out to be the cause of our progress later on.

> A person was constantly praying for progress and success in his career. But he saw that whenever he prayed, his problems at the workplace grew all the more. Disputes and arguments with colleagues and managers went on the rise. Seeing this, he became apprehensive and stopped praying. After some days, he resumed praying for growth. Again, the same incidents repeated. This time, matters took a turn for the worse and he was expelled from his job.
>
> A few days later, he went to another town in search of a new job. Incidentally, he met an old friend there. He told him that he was in search of a job. His friend exclaimed, "There is a vacancy in my company that exactly matches your profile! And they want somebody who is not already having a job. You can definitely apply." Delighted, he applied for the job and got it. Soon, his hard work, dedication and sincerity opened the doors of success for him. He was amazed at his own progress and realized that he had been praying for exactly such a job.

Thus you see how presumptions can become obstacles in the fulfillment of your prayers. The full secret of prayer makes you realize that the result of your prayer may not come in the form that you have envisaged.

3. Ego

If you are unaware of the full secret of prayer, it may lead to the rise of ego. And if ego is present, it is not possible to attract higher things in life. Ego can attract things only at lower planes of consciousness. The human ego is unaware that there is something bigger and more powerful than it. Ego makes one blind to the things one can actually receive in life through prayer. Ego leaves one satisfied with very little, when so much more is actually available in nature. Hence, the need is to surrender the ego to God and enjoy the benefits of grace that God wants to shower on you.

4. Contradictory prayers

A significant missing link that we need to bear in mind is that every thought that is imbued with feeling is a prayer. Many people believe that prayer is limited to the few minutes that one folds one's hands before a chosen deity and asks for what one wishes.

We are constantly praying when we are thinking. The thoughts that we entertain are nothing but prayers. The universe is constantly listening to what we are transmitting. Hence, it is very important to be aware of the kind of thoughts that we entertain. It is quite likely that we may be entertaining thoughts that contradict our conscious prayers. As a result, the two thoughts cancel each other out. These are known as contradictory prayers.

A person may pray that he grows in his career; he may seek a promotion in his organization to the post of a divisional manager. A post may become available, perhaps in a different town. However, he also thinks that he should remain in his hometown. He may be reluctant to travel away from his home. You can see that his prayer for promotion could have borne fruit, but gets cancelled out by his reluctance to travel.

Be in Meditation to Receive Answers to Prayers

In the context of manifesting a good life, if prayer is the question, then meditation is the answer! Prayer is only half the secret of creating what you aspire. Meditation completes the secret. Meditation is the full secret. People focus on prayer, on creative visualization and manifestation techniques based on the law of attraction. But they miss the all-important need to meditate. You ask for something through prayer. But then you have to be in silence to receive the answer. In other words, being in meditation makes you receptive and attuned to the creative principle, so as to receive what you have prayed for. This is a missing link.

> **Full-secret**
>
> Ask through Prayer and be in the state of meditation to receive answers.

Meditation helps in creating the right state within you, which can help you receive what you have prayed for. Before anything is to be given to man, he is made to pray for it. Meditation creates a state of emptiness within him. So long as this emptiness is not created within, man cannot receive what he needs. Meditation creates that space within you to receive the object of your prayer.

Discussions on the law of attraction and manifestation focus on the principle of prayer. However, they fall short of explaining the deeper truth of how prayer is fulfilled. They do not satisfactorily answer how we can experience a life of permanent and boundless bliss. They provide only the half-secret to leading a life of bliss and fulfillment.

Being able to manifest what you desire does not necessarily guarantee lasting happiness. This is the missing link in the practice of manifestation techniques based on the law of attraction. Without understanding this missing link, it is common for people to get into frenzy with manifesting their desires by using the power of thoughts, using focused imagination techniques, believing that it would deliver lasting happiness.

Since thoughts and feelings are used as the key to manifesting what we desire in life, we rarely get the thought of going beyond this and accessing the Source of thoughts and feelings. Those who have been able to unlock the full-secret of thoughts have attained the ultimate treasure of life. They have reveled in the experience of boundless bliss, unconditional love, and unbroken peace. They have expressed the highest creation of life.

Meditation is the state in which we access the source of all creation. We access and abide in the state of pure consciousness, from where thoughts arise. It is the state of silent stillness from where creation originates.

Imagine a scene where a little child is playing with his toys. Some of the toys are broken, some are scattered. His clothes, toys, schoolbag, pens and books are all scattered. But when the child goes to sleep, his mother comes and tidies the place, neatly arranging everything. How did the child help the situation? By being quiet and sleeping.

We also need to emulate the little child. We may be surrounded by problem situations, by unfulfilled desires. By being in the quietude of pure silence, we allow pure consciousness to set everything right. We allow our highest potential to unfold when we are in the stillness of meditation. Our prayers, that we have passed earlier, move towards fruition.

When we place an order at a restaurant, the bearer proceeds to arrange the food for us. However, if we keep calling the bearer repeatedly and keep ordering, he will never find the time to fulfill our orders. Hence, it is important to give the bearer the time to fetch the order.

In the same way, when we are constantly engaged in ceaseless thinking, we don't give our prayers the space to move into manifestation. Meditation brings us into a receptive state where the answers to our prayers begin to move towards us.

Does this mean we need to sit down in a proper posture, close our eyes and remain still for a period of time after praying? While this ritual is definitely essential to get into the state of meditation, here we are talking about the sustenance of such a state even while sitting, standing, walking, eating, talking, working, etc. After you pray and enjoy the experience of meditation, you also need to sustain it after getting up and going about your daily life.

Meditation is a state in which you strengthen your faith, purify your mind, remain established in the present, develop your patience, and build conviction on the laws of nature that govern how prayer works. If you remain in a state of meditation after prayer, it brings the highest possibility to manifest.

Let us consider each of these five aspects that unfold with meditation.

1. Faith

Meditation is a state in which your faith in the divine purpose of life is established. Faith is the greatest vibration on earth. Being in this vibration attracts the best possibilities. Your prayers bear fruit only due to the releasing of faith hidden within you. You get an experience of this faith every now and then. Often after an event has occurred we hear people exclaim, "I knew this would happen! I was sure of it." Thus even with the release of a little faith, you feel so happy. Just imagine the miracles that will happen when all of your faith gets a release!

2. Purity of mind

Being in the state of meditation purifies the mind. The purer your mind, the cleaner are your vibrations. If you harbor malice, hatred or jealousy, unconsciously you attract negative things into your own life. This is a simple law of nature.

3. Being in the present

The unprepared mind generally tends to vacillate in the past or future. When you are in the present, you simply follow your instinctive, intuitive thought process that is required for going about your daily work. It is in such a state that you become receptive to cues from nature in response to your prayers. If you act upon these cues, you gravitate towards the thing you have asked for.

4. Understanding

Sometimes, God is so pleased with our sincere prayers that He wishes for us to receive greater things than those we have asked for. We need to understand this divine arrangement; hence 'understanding' is an important aspect of the state of meditation.

For example, a person once undertook hard penance to appease Lakshmi – the Goddess of wealth. But the Goddess did not appear before him. He was very disappointed. In that state, he set off in search of the ultimate truth. After some years of seeking, he finally attained the truth. He was in a state of bliss. It was then that the Goddess appeared before him. When the person exclaimed that he no longer needed wealth, because he had gained something far greater than wealth, the Goddess revealed that it was with this purpose that She had not appeared before him earlier. She was so pleased with his prayers that she wished for things greater than wealth for him.

Thus the state of meditation entails the understanding that whatever we are praying for is definitely getting answered; we must only be able to understand these answers. Our prayers could well be arising from ignorance or based on a limited understanding. Meditation prepares us to receive higher answers to our limited prayers.

Hence, the prayer that arises from higher understanding is: 'O God, I may ask for various things that are not in my best interest due to my limited understanding; but please grant me what you feel is best for me.'

5. Patience and courage

Once you pray for something with faith, love and purity of mind, there is nothing other than your own thoughts that can stop it from coming to you. Your own doubts, suspicions, fears, imaginations and presumptions put a block in its path. Hence patience and courage are important virtues that you must keep while in a state of meditation.

Patience is a virtue that enables us to wait for the right time for our prayers to be answered. It lends us the courage to tide through situations when our prayers are not answered. After all, we learn and mature more when our prayers are not answered!

THE HIGHEST PRAYER

Prayer is also offered before meditation as it helps us to enter the receptive state of meditation. But the greatest prayer commences when we are fully immersed in the state of inner stillness in meditation. Abiding in that state of silent receptivity is the ultimate prayer beyond words. When a body enters that state, it becomes fully receptive to the Source of everything. The mere presence of such pure being is the greatest prayer for the universe.

Thus, being in the state of meditation is the ultimate prayer. When you consider this perspective, prayer and meditation are both the same. From the other perspective, you begin with prayer and culminate in meditation. You ask through prayer and receive through meditation. It depends on how we look at it.

2
Beyond Virtuousness

We find people with different dispositions. Some are very active, always engaged in action, while there are others who are sedentary, lethargic and inactive. What drives their dispositions? Is it true that some people are pre-disposed to more action while others aren't?

Let us first explore what has been said so far about human expression – the half secret. According to modern science, everything in the universe is made of energy. The human body too is like a vortex of energy. But what is it that drives this energy to express in a variety of ways? What determines the variety of human temperaments?

One of the fascinating discoveries that the ancient and time-tested system of yoga has expounded is how the human embodiment is governed by its three major attributes – *Sattva*, *Rajas* and *Tamas*. These three *gunas* (qualities, temperaments) determine the disposition of the human body-mind. The play of these three temperaments is subtle and unseen, but their expression is perceivable at all levels of human existence – physical, mental, intellectual and occupational.

Tamas is the tendency of inertia or passivity. *Rajas* is the tendency of movement or activity. *Sattva* is the tendency of equanimity or balance. The proportion of these three temperaments within the human body-mind shapes its overall behavior. This is why you find people prone to a variety of dispositions.

Tamas is characterized by lethargy, inertia, passivity, ignorance, greed and attachment to lowly desires. Tamasic people tend to prefer stale or preserved food; they somehow don't like fresh and wholesome food. They are laid-back and find solace in pleasures that stimulate their senses. A tamasic mind indulges in base thoughts and negative emotions like hatred, anger and ill-will. A tamasic intellect is dull and rigid.

A tamasic body is prone to lethargy. If they find that something can be done in sleeping position instead of a sitting, they prefer the sleeping position. If something can be done in a sitting position instead of standing, they prefer to sit. And if something can take them from one place to another without having to walk, they prefer that option. 'Rest' is their topmost priority in any activity they do.

Rajas is the quality that fuels activity. It serves as an engine for life-in-action. However, when this engine goes into overdrive, the result is hyperactivity. Rajasic people find it difficult to relax, both physically and mentally. They have to be constantly engaged in some activity. They typically prefer hot and spicy food, which they eat quickly. They are always focused on what they should do next.

They are highly ambitious, whether or not they have the qualities to achieve them. They are rarely satisfied with whatever they have, and constantly seek new sensations and variety in life.

Rajasic people just cannot stay still, both physically and mentally. Even if they are forced to sit at one place, they keep moving around. It is easy to notice that they are the other extreme of tamasic people.

Sattva is the quality of equanimity and balance. It is the most subtle and intangible of the three gunas. Sattva expresses as composure, level-headedness, purity and virtuousness. Sattva-predominant people eat to live; they don't live to eat. They are sensitive to the effects of food on the body and mind. They always eat a well-balanced and optimum quantity of food. They do not overindulge in any one thing. They tread the middle path.

Sattvic people make optimum use of sleep, activity and rest. They tread the path of balance between work and rest. Consider that the human heart beats around 72 times a minute on average, but also relaxes 72 times a minute. Due to this balance of work and rest, it can ceaselessly function for a very long time, sometimes for even more than hundred years. Sattva-predominant people are privy to this secret and emulate this example of the heart. They rest before they get tired and resume activity before lethargy sets in.

It is possible to have a mix of these tendencies at different levels of existence. For example, one who has a predominantly tamasic body can have a predominantly rajasic mind. Such a person will always be lost in incessant thinking and emotional sways while being physically sluggish.

Progressing Towards Being Sattvic

Being sattvic helps in making progress on the spiritual path. The sattvic attributes of balance and equanimity render the mind and body to be more receptive to subtler wisdom. A sattvic intellect is capable of grasping subtle nuances of the truth of life. The mind is tranquil and more attuned to get into a deep meditative state.

> ### Half-secret
> Aim to be of *sattvic* nature by developing virtuous qualities of *sattva* (equanimity and balance).

Everyone would love to become sattvic after getting to know its virtues. All the three *gunas* are present in everyone in varying proportions. It's not that sattva is totally absent in tamas or rajas predominant people. Some amount of sattva is active even in the most tamasic or rajasic people. It's just that it has been muted because they have constantly ignored it in favour of tamas or rajas. Constantly ignoring the sattvic force within your body-mind makes it dormant.

But is it possible to inculcate the sattvic quality? Can we become sattvic if we're pre-disposed to a predominantly tamasic or rajasic nature? Yes, it is very much within us to raise the *guna* we want.

The secret to develop sattva is to inculcate wholesome habits that promote sattva. For example, one can begin with eating habits. An oft-repeated saying is that you are what you eat. Program your mind to enjoy easily digestible, nutritious and energizing food. Cross out heavy, fatty, spicy, sugary, processed and preserved food. When you begin with reforming the habits of your body, your mind too follows suit. You will become more receptive to the changes you need to make in your lifestyle.

When we begin to make progress and raise our sattvic quotient, we automatically receive signals and cues from nature about what to do next. Act upon the cues, develop and ingrain your newly acquired habits. Soon, you will find yourself enjoying a sattvic lifestyle.

However, here's a word of caution – Being sattvic is not the ultimate goal of life. There are dangers of remaining stuck with a sattvic way of life without seeking to go beyond it. And this is where the full secret needs unraveling.

Transcending the Three *Gunas*

The understanding of the full secret brings a paradigm shift in how we can approach our human mechanism.

To be able to understand the state beyond sattva, it is essential to first understand that these *gunas* are the qualities of your body, mind and intellect; they are not *your* qualities. You are not your body, mind or intellect. Your true nature is pure consciousness – the real Self. The Self presides over the body, mind and intellect. You are not subservient to your *gunas*; you are their master. It is you who ought to take control of them and not the other way round.

The state that is beyond the three *gunas* is known as the *Guna-ateet* state (*ateet* = beyond) – the state that transcends these dispositions of your body-mind mechanism. It can also be called as the trans-sattvic state where one goes beyond the sattvic disposition. Being in the *Gunateet* state, you can put the three *gunas* to effective use for Self-expression, without being susceptible to their influence.

Dangers of Remaining Stuck with Sattva Guna

Following a sattvic way of life is good, as long as you are willing to consciously progress beyond it. It is necessary to move from 'good' to 'God' – from being virtuous to merging with divinity.

> **Full-secret**
>
> Transcend the three *Gunas* and abide in the *Gunateet* state beyond equanimity, activity and inertia. A sattvic way of life is not good enough if you stop at it without progressing further.

Many people who take to spirituality consider the progression to a sattvic way of life as the final goal. There are dangers inherent in resting on the plateau of sattva, without transcending it. The biggest danger of remaining stuck with sattva is the probability of backsliding into tamas. If sattvic people are unaware that there is something beyond sattva, they can become complacent, egoistic and arrogant.

While sattvic people do a lot of good for society, their benevolence can also boost their ego. There is no harm in doing selfless service, as long as they are truly selfless. People of sattvic nature tend to take credit for performing altruistic deeds for the wellbeing of society. True wisdom lies in surrendering all deeds to the real Self. However, they revel in a sense of self-pride for being the doer of noble deeds.

Being bound to negative or malevolent deeds is like being bound by iron handcuffs. However, being attached to virtuous deeds is like being bound to golden handcuffs. Even if they are golden, they are handcuffs after all… they bind you. One cannot easily discern this subtle form of bondage. While avoiding negative deeds is good, being attached to positive deeds can also stall your progress. Sattva-predominant people need to progress by transcending both – negative and positive deeds.

The other danger in being sattvic is the belief that says, "I know it all." People who have the arrogance of "I know it all" can get trapped in the mire of sattva. They tend to be lost in intellectual delights and flaunt their knowledge of spirituality. Such knowledge is mere information, not true wisdom. True progress happens only when one becomes empty off all notions and abides like an empty flute, through which divine music can be played.

It can be considered unfortunate for someone who has come near the ultimate state to then backslide due to complacency or arrogance. It would be sad because this person had overcome tamas and rajas and had the momentum to transcend the gunas.

Characters from Hindu mythology like Yudhishtira and Lord Indra serve as examples of those stuck with sattva. Hindu mythology symbolizes Lord Indra as the lord of rains. People would gather and pray to him if they didn't receive adequate rainfall. Indra is shown as being surrounded by beautiful angels and *apsaras*, which is symbolic of the fruit of being sattvic. Enamored with his wonderful state, he forgets to shed rain on Earth. Consequently, he is dethroned and slips into tamas, as a result of which he has to restart his journey towards sattva.

Hence it is essential to access the *Gunateet* state and abide in it.

The *Gunateet* State

Pure Consciousness transcends the three temperaments; you are pure consciousness. When you abide in the detached state of pure consciousness, you can choose when to use tamas, when to use rajas, and when to use sattva.

For example, you make use of tamas to get into deep sleep at bedtime. While meditating you make controlled use of tamas and sattva to enter into deep state of stillness. When some activity needs to be done, you make use of rajas and perform the activity. Thus, for everything that you need to do, you have your gunas at your disposal.

If the need is to get up and do something, you actuate rajas and start doing it. You are aware that you are employing the guna for the divine purpose of your body-mind; hence you don't get attached to it. You experience yourself as the detached witnesser of all activity. You recognize that you are not defined by your gunas. You clearly see your gunas as mere tools and choose them; the tools don't control you. You make a wise decision every time because you are not swayed by your temperaments. This is true Self-mastery.

The *Gunateet* state doesn't distance you from the world. You take part in every activity that you need to. Inspired actions arise from the Self and express through your body-mind. It is just that although you are very much part of everything, but you are not attached to it. You connect and transact with the world with an indifferent curiosity. You have a top-view of things. You express divine love for people; not 'personalized' love that is related to the body and mind. Every activity becomes a means of Self-expression instead of fuelling the ego. Thus the gunateet state is a state of freedom and liberation.

Shifting to the *Gunateet* State

The *Gunateet* state exists beyond all effort. It is our true nature. When we assume ourselves to be the body-mind, we are attached to the body-mind and consumed by the play of the gunas. Hence, shifting to the transcendental state is about recognizing our true nature. With the right understanding of the nature of Self, we can learn to abide in pure untouched awareness, from where we can witness the continuous flux of the gunas.

While we work to gain clear recognition of our true nature, we can start by raising our awareness to spot the play of tamas, rajas and sattva in daily life. With higher awareness, we can spot it when the three gunas are at work within us. Sattva needs to be given priority because it is the bridge towards the *Gunateet* state.

Consider the situation when you feel like sitting in meditation. If you are sattva-predominant, you will immediately go ahead and remain seated in meditation. But if you are tamas or rajas predominant, you might feel like procrastinating. You might think, "Let's do it later; not now." Spot the rise of tamas or rajas here. If you feel like sleeping instead of meditating, tamas is at work. If you feel like watching your favorite TV show or getting into activity, rajas is at work. We need to spot this with higher awareness.

When you feel like meditating, it is a force from the Self that you need to use to go within. If you allow tamas or rajas to take over, you are in effect using "force against force." Instead of submitting yourself to the positive force of sattva, you act against it and give way to tamas or rajas. We need to become alert to the play of the *gunas*.

With the guidance of a true Guru, you can move from tamas to sattva but also beyond sattva into the stateless transcendental state of Self-awareness.

3

True Love – The Wellspring Within You

Most people, these days, lead a superficial life; they live at the surface of the ocean of life. The ever-increasing pace of life and the constant barrage from media sources lead to an ever-reducing attention span. People do not have the time to pause and dip into the deeper experience of what it means to be alive, of what it really means to be connected with people. They are lost to the experience of real joy that is hidden behind the surface of friendships or relationships.

If you see what's going on in the Facebook accounts of many people, you will realize that they are merely 'Surface-book' accounts. People wish to make themselves known to others through a Surface-book. They observe the surface traits that can make them popular and accordingly create an avatar (self-image) of themselves, which they advertise in their social circles.

How can they make themselves known to others when they don't know themselves—the essence of who-they-truly-are? For that, they will have to take a dip below the surface to discover the vastness of the ocean of their true being. Those who have dived deep into the ocean within can tell you how blissful and peaceful our reality is.

BEYOND PHYSICAL APPEARANCES

There are many who get enamored by physical appearances, by temporary aspects, which make them attached to people. They don't even realize when the love for their near and dear ones turns into attachment. They live in the illusion that such attachment is love.

Such attachment leads to infatuation, lust, the need to gratify the senses and greed. People bind themselves in conditional behavior that is vulnerable to feelings like jealousy, possessiveness, suspicion and doubts. Such a form of base love exists in the physical plane. The underlying belief here is that we *are* our physical bodies.

> **Half-secret**
>
> True love transcends physical appearances and looks deeper at the mind and heart of people.

There are also many, who have realized that appearances are ephemeral. Appearances come and go. They realize the importance of looking through surface aspects and establishing a sound foundation for relationships based on lasting aspects like mental virtues and shared values. They experience love that is beyond the body. They appreciate the mental and intellectual traits of a person to love them.

Philosophers encourage others to appreciate and love the inner beauty of people rather than their physical or wealth attributes. A person's nature and inner personality is more important than external looks. With this higher form of love, we love people for what they are "made of." This kind of love is mostly in the mental plane. The underlying belief in such love is that we are the mind and intellect.

But this is only the half-secret. The personality or individual that we love is only the surface. True love is love that lives deep below the surface. What lies beneath the surface is oneness; oneness of all creations. The same consciousness resides in each one of us; the same energy expresses itself through each one of us. On the outside we may all look different but the truth is that we all exist in the same inner experience.

True love exists in the awareness of this oneness. This oneness is our true Self; the universal Self, the real 'I'. We have all experienced this oneness at some point or the other. We have all experienced it as infants. As infants we were literally swimming deep in the ocean of true love, as we knew no 'other'. But now we have risen to the surface. Our purpose now is to re-enter the ocean and stabilize in it.

The Disillusionment of Personalized Love

In the physical world, the mirror shows us our reflections... the faces that appear before the mirror may keep changing, but the mirror remains the same. But the higher truth of spirituality is that the face (the real Self) remains the same. Mirrors keep changing! The mirrors here refer to the several bodies through which the real Self – the pure consciousness – manifests. The same face (of the universal Self) is being reflected in all the mirrors (bodies).

In the rainy season, you see puddles being formed on earth that get filled with the rainwater. The moon is reflected in all the puddles. It is as if there are several moons. But the real moon is only one. The same moon is shining in each puddle. Each puddle only serves to reflect the same moon. In the same way, it is the one Self that is looking out, whether it is through your body-mind, or through the body-mind of the other person.

The real quest within each one of us is to reach the true face – the face of the Self – the experience of who-we-truly-are. But there are so many layers in between that conceal this truth. The illusion of 'many' is the fundamental deception. The mental layers that form on this deception are the beliefs and expectations that we nurture around this illusion of 'many'. To the extent that there are mental layers of separateness and individuality, to that extent we deal only at the surface level – body-to-body, mind-to-mind, individual-to-individual, Facebook-to-Facebook in the virtual 'surface' world!

People never consciously go deeper to unravel the real face. And yet, unknowingly, they do touch deep at the real face… and that's when they feel true unconditional love, be it any relationship. It could be the love of the mother for her son, of the son for his father, of the lover for his beloved, it could be the love of the brother for his sister, of the sister for her brother. In relationships, when love rises up to being unconditional, one gets the glimpse of the real face.

When people sing about the magic of beholding the beloved, what is the magic in it? When one beholds the other in true love, one doesn't realize that one is beholding the face of the real Self, looking out from within that body. It is the same face that is peeping out from within oneself. In other words, one catches a wondrous glimpse of one's own Self through the other person. At least for a few moments, he catches a glimpse of that deeper truth – the real face behind all faces.

When one experiences a glimpse of the real Self through connectedness in any relationship, one longs for this glimpse again and again. One is drawn towards that particular person, that individual, in whom he or she was able to witness the face of the real Self. This happens in ignorance of the real secret that the other person has only given a glimpse of one's own face. When you feel unconditional love for anyone, they are giving you a glimpse of your true face… your true Self. Deep within, you have been constantly seeking your own face… your own Self… everywhere… in all other faces.

The Self is the source of love… it is love, bliss and peace in essence. Even the pleasure that one seeks in the external world is actually the pursuit for the bliss that exists within oneself. But due to the illusion of multiple faces, one begins to feel that one is experiencing joy because of being in the company of a particular person, a particular individual. When this belief is reinforced that your joy comes from being with certain people, then you try to fix their company. You try to sustain their presence in your life. You keep trying to ensure that the one in whose presence you have experienced joy and love will remain with you forever.

One feels insecure that this bond that gave the experience of pure love should not be lost. Hence one tries to lock the other person and capture the other person's presence in an attempt to quell this feeling of insecurity. And it is this very attempt to hold and fix the person in a relationship that becomes its undoing.

The magic begins to evaporate when people encounter the layers at the surface… the individual persona. The real face of pure love that they had glimpsed gets hidden behind this surface of the individual persona. One then tries to emulate the love artificially, but it doesn't give the real fulfillment. Doubts and disillusionment take over. The moment one gets the slightest hint that this person can move away, one begins to experience sorrow.

Understanding True Love

The word 'Love' has been corrupted through misuse to such an extent that we, as a society, have lost its essential meaning. What is true love?

Just as space permeates everything in the universe, love permeates every part, every aspect of creation. If there is one answer to the question, "How and why does this world exist?" the answer, in one word, is 'Love'. Rather, the answer is 'Pure Love', since the word 'love' has lost its meaning.

Your very existence is an expression of pure unconditional love of the Source (you may call it Consciousness, Creator, God, Divine

Self, or any other name). This is the truth of your being. True love transcends both love and hatred. It is unconditional, unquestioning, boundless, unchanging love. It is overflowing love of the Source for the Source *through* all of creation.

True love is way beyond the personalized love that two or more individuals assert on one another. It has nothing to do with emotions like attachment, attraction, craving, or infatuation that is felt by individuals. Personalized love, though apparently selfless, is rooted in desires and conditional satisfaction.

While unpleasant emotions like anger, hatred or sorrow are considered as negative feelings, people assume attachment (disguised as love) to be a positive virtue. Between two people who are in so-called love, the feelings of jealousy or possessiveness are also misconstrued as love. There cannot be a greater corruption than this.

We have been brought up in a society that judges love based on conditions. Almost all of us have been raised in a belief-system of conditional love. We have been taught that love is something to be earned. We have been made to believe that we can receive love only when we fit into people's expectations. If we are not good enough, we will be deprived of love. If someone does not love us back, they don't deserve our love.

These beliefs have influenced the collective psyche of families, groups, communities, and societies since generations to such an extent that love has been reduced to fear of denial. While love is the all-pervasive essence of everything, such false notions of love have caused fear to be perpetuated into of our lives.

We need to shift from the paradigm of false conditional love to the essence of pure unconditional love. The question is: How do we get to experience pure unconditional love? And the answer is: by eliminating the ego – the false 'I' – that we assume for our persona. As long as we believe that whatever is inside the skin is 'me' and whatever is outside the skin is 'not me', we cannot experience true love.

One who considers oneself separate from others will remain floating on the surface. You can see waves rising in the ocean. If the waves start thinking that they are separate from one another, what will you say? You would say that they are in an illusion that they are separate. The reality is that they all are the ocean; they are an expression of the ocean.

The experience of true love comes with surrender of the false 'I', in letting go of the feeling of separateness. Without this sacrifice, it is not possible to attain divine love. When this separate 'I' is discarded, you embrace everything in oneness and catch a glimpse of pure love. You realize that this is what you were really seeking all the time, behind all pursuits.

This is the full secret – The real pursuit behind all relationships is to experience the loving essence of who-you truly-are. This may not seem obvious to start with.

Stop Holding Onto Past Impressions

We have a habit of creating a 'packet' (impression) of each experience and storing this packet in memory. When the next experience comes, we unconsciously refer the previous packet and compare its taste with the present taste. When we find the taste to be dissimilar, we reject the new experience and lose out on its uniqueness.

For example, when we experience true love in a relationship, we think that this person is a perfect match for us. We store a mental packet about the specific behavior that led us to like the person. But as soon as the person does something that contradicts this packet, our love for the person begins to dwindle. For example, the person may present some other person with a gift but forget to gift us. If such incidents keep repeating, the new behavior hurts us as we compare it with likable experiences that we have packeted earlier.

This habit of holding onto past impressions can cause so much frustration that it can even lead to breakups. People break apart and look for love in new associations. But again, the same thing repeats and they continue to believe that the fault lies in the people. They hop from person to person, but never realize why they got to experience pure love in the first place. It was because the mind was empty without any past impressions!

Many people say that it is hard to forget their first love. And everyone else agrees with them. But has anybody given a thought as to why this happens? With the first love, they had no previous packets of that experience. Hence, they simply loved that experience in its uniqueness. But then they created such packets that any following experiences seemed bland thereafter. Therefore the need is to develop the quality of not creating packets of past impressions. Experience each moment as if it is the first time.

The Guiding Principle of Love

When we understand the full secret of love, the guiding principle of love also becomes clear to us:

True love can be experienced only through giving, not by demanding. People who exist in your life are not here to love you. They are here to remind you that you are the Source of Love.

Full-secret
The real pursuit behind all relationships is to experience the loving essence of who-you truly-are. You are the Source of Love.

Logical reasoning suggests that we can have something only when we obtain it. Many people live with the belief that we can experience love only when we acquire it. Howsoever illogical as it may sound, the experience of pure love does not lie in acquiring, but rather in giving it unconditionally. If you receive love, it is merely a bonus.

Love by its nature is giving. It gives boundlessly when it is brimming in life. Everything we see and experience is the expression of love. When you experience true love, you only feel like giving overwhelmingly and unconditionally. It feels great to expect nothing in return!

However, without knowing this, man spends his entire lifetime in seeking love, which often eludes him or her. He keeps yearning for appreciation, for consideration, for approval from people.

For example, someone, who has worked hard all through his work life before retirement and never received any appreciation, breaks down into tears when his colleagues speak good things about him at his farewell. He has waited all those years to hear a few words of praise or approval. Not being aware of how true love works has caused him to seek love from the external world.

You can never find true and everlasting love in the external world. Whenever you find yourself feeling deprived of love, you need to remind yourself about this truth. By knowing that you are the Source of love, you can love yourself, instead of waiting to receive love from the world. Ask yourself, "Why do I need an agent to love myself?" Waiting for the world to love you, is like hiring an agent to love yourself!

It is time for you to honor yourself as the Source of love. You have undertaken this human journey to realize and express the boundless love that you truly are. When you entertain emotions like fear and guilt, you are not honoring your true nature of pure love. If you truly love yourself, you will never want to hurt yourself through such negative emotions.

Deal with the Source, Not the Channels

When man receives anything, he mistakenly assumes the channel through which he receives to be the Source. As a result, he expects to receive further from the same channel and becomes disheartened if the channel does not deliver the goods.

For example, if his brother, who used to help him earlier, stops helping him, he says, "My brother has let me down." If his father does not assign a share of his property to the son, then the son starts hating his father. This is so because people assume their relatives to be the givers, the Source.

This is true even for love. We ignorantly invite sorrow when we get habituated to desire love from specific people around us. When we need water, we draw it from the tap. But the tap does not have any capacity of giving. It is merely a channel for the water source. There are many taps (channels) through which water is received, but they all come from the same water reservoir (source). When we insist that we want to be loved only by a particular person, we invite sorrow in our lives.

If you seek the experience of love directly from the Source, you will get more than you could ever ask for. You give up your limited perspective of expecting from a particular person. You will realize that there are many channels through which the Source can give. Everything is in abundance in the Source. It is common sense to expect from the Source, rather than the channels.

Further, when you go beyond expecting love, you reach the understanding that the Source is expressing *through* you. You become the channel for unconditional love to flow through you. Your dealings in daily life are with the Source alone. You stop dealing with individuals and begin to see the Source in them. You honor the Source who functions through them. You give to the Source and receive from the Source through all your dealings. You will not expect from individuals as you rest in faith that everything that has to come, will come from the Source.

Loving Every Aspect of the World

Pure love makes it possible for you to unconditionally love yourself first, so that you have the strength to shower love on others. In fact, when you express love by being the Source, you naturally love the Source *in* others.

Every aspect of the world is an expression of God's will. Out of ignorance, we love one part of this world while refusing to accept the other part. Out of fear, we do not embrace the world in its wholeness. By judging or hating the world for its imperfections, we create more of what we judge or hate. All the imperfections that we perceive are actually a shadow cast by our refusal to lovingly accept whatever is.

Pure love is always from the Source for the Source. It is not based on external conditions. It is an illusion if people appear good due to attachment or at fault due to aversion. In reality, from the standpoint of the Source, everyone is faultless; everything exists in perfection. When you see faults in them, you cannot love them. Pure love is experienced when you see the world as a beautiful and faultless expression of the creator.

4

Living in the Present

Don't many of us wish to change our past? It would be nice if we could, wouldn't it? All our remorse would be gone. We would become what we had always dreamt of. We would get rid of our mistakes, misjudgments, spoiled relations and what not. But it is crazy to think that way. Everyone knows that it is just not possible to change the things that have already happened. Yet, many of us ruminate over the past and imagine how life would be if things had been different.

It is the same with the future. We either fantasize about the future or get scared of it and worry about it. However much we think about it or hope for something to happen, the reality is that the future is merely a projection of our present. This doesn't mean that we shouldn't plan or dream for a future. It is just that we need to understand that the only time we can ever change is the present.

Most people fail to achieve their goals in the future because they are entangled in the tendencies that they have developed in the past. Remorse, sadness, worry, fear, anxiety and stress are all a result of vacillating between the past and the future, and failing to be in the present moment.

> ### Half-secret
>
> Focus on the present moment to avoid vacillating in the past and future. Present is the instant between past and future.

The secret of getting rid of such feelings is to focus on the present moment, to live in the present. When you live in the present, you are least concerned of what has happened in the past and what might happen in the future. It is only in the present that you have the reins of your life in your own hands. You can take control of your future only in the present. You can overcome regrets and past memories only in the present.

Did you know that airplanes and ships spend 90% of time off course? Winds and water currents constantly push them in one direction or the other. The job of the captain is to keep correcting the direction of the airplane or ship and aim it at the final destination. You are the captain of your life. Winds of the past and future will keep pushing you off course. But by staying in the present, you have the controls firmly in your hands. In the present, you can steer your course and move towards your final destination.

The Present Moment – The Gift of Life

The present moment is the stuff of life. 'Now' is the gift of life, spreading its wings. True peace can be experienced only in the present moment. There are innumerable secondary benefits of living in the present. It has a dramatic effect on our emotional wellbeing, because it is a great stress buster to cut out thoughts of the past and anxiety of the future. Consequently, it also positively impacts our physical health. Living in the present improves creativity. It makes us appreciate the world more, because we no longer have time for judging and criticizing. It boosts our productivity because we stop worrying about things other than the job at hand. Most importantly, living in the present opens us up to see and experience life without preconceived notions. Things start flowing easier through us, because of the lifting of barriers from within our mind.

However, the present moment seems fleeting to us. It seems like such a short moment that it can be very hard to catch hold of it. Although many people know the importance of living in the present, they find it impossible to do so. One of the reasons for this is that they're constantly talking to themselves mentally. The present moment is lost in mental chatter. How can one ever manage to find the present moment? How can one enjoy what's in front of them and 'smell the coffee' as they say?

But there is more. The real reason why people find it difficult to be in the present is that they think that the present is 'time'. They think that the moment between the past and the future, on the time scale, is the present. And here is where the full secret comes in to quell this great misconception.

The Spacious Present – Beyond Time

To understand the missing link, we need to first look deeply at the dimension called 'time'.

Time is a dimension that enables us to make sense of this phenomenal world. It is an essential element of the manifest universe. Time exists only when the world exists. The words 'before' and 'after' are facets of linear time. It cannot explain what exists beyond time. Consciousness – the undifferentiated state of the true Self is beyond time.

You may call it Self, or Consciousness, or God, Allah, Christ, *Ishwar*, or the Divine Presence. All these words point at the same living essence, which precedes the world. When one stabilizes in the experience of the Self, one realizes that there is neither a 'past' nor a 'future'. The eternal present alone is. The so-called past and future are experienced in the timeless present. This is beyond the grasp of the intellect.

Let us imagine that there are some transparent photo films containing certain images. If ten such photo films are stacked together and we look at the entire stack, we will not be able to understand the images, because they overlap. To understand each picture, we will need a gap between the photographs and watch them one after the other. The effect created by this gap is called 'time'.

Time is such a wondrous aspect of creation. It enables you to watch and understand the living pictures of the manifest world in sequence. Just because the element of time is brought in, the eternal 'now' gets divided into 'past', 'present' and 'future'. Time is thus a method of seeing the entire film of life in a particular sequence. Otherwise, the entire film is happening in the here-and-now.

You can either think about the present moment, or just be the present. When you attempt to capture the present moment in your thoughts, it eludes you. The mind insists, "I want to grasp the present moment. I want to know how it is like." This wish becomes a hurdle in just being the present.

Past is memory and the future is imagination. Past and future exist merely in thoughts that arise in the timeless present. Hence, the mind has this mistaken notion that the present also can be grasped in terms of thoughts. You experience the timeless eternal present when you see thoughts for what they truly are, without being consumed by the content of the thoughts.

Full-secret

> Transcend thoughts to enter the eternal present – the space in which past and future exist. Present is the vast space behind the past-future continuum.

The present is not an instant between the past and future that can be captured by thinking. This is the missing link that many fail to see. The Present is the space in which the past and future appear as thoughts.

Your essential nature is Consciousness. It can be experienced as the living presence in which everything is being known. This presence is beyond time and space. The world appears like waves on the surface of the ocean of pure silence. All forms and phenomena arise and dissolve in this eternal silence. Even thoughts are like waves that arise from and dissolve into this silence.

Thus, the full secret is that the present is not time; it is the spacious presence in which everything comes into being. The moment between the past and the future on the scale of time is not the present. The present moment is merely the window through which you enter the spacious present. This space exists behind the scale of time. In fact, this space is omnipresent. It is the base for all of the time scale. The feeling in the space of present is that of timelessness. This space is divine space; it can be said that this is where God truly lives!

Shifting Into the Present Space

It is the mind that creates the illusion of time. The mind feels remorseful of past events and wishes that things were different. It entertains itself with past memories and wishes to relive them. It fears for the future. It fantasizes about the future. It constantly grumbles about something or the other. It judges things and compares new experiences with past experiences. Preoccupied with such activities, it fails to experience the fresh present. It lives either in the past or the future, creating the illusion of time.

If this mind falls silent, we enter the space of the present. In this space, the mind doesn't come and check whether we are indeed in the present. It doesn't come and check whether God is also present in this space. It doesn't judge new experiences based on past experiences. It doesn't compare present experiences with past ones. It does not imagine what the experience would be like. In the space of the present, we have totally surrendered our mind. We simply live each moment and enjoy every experience in its raw form. We view the world as it is, without the spectacles of preconceived notions, just like a baby newly arrived in the world.

When we are purely in the present, we are established in our heart, not in our head. The head can only contain thoughts of the present, but the heart *is* the present! Establishing ourselves in the present is the shift from head to heart.

The space of the present covers the entire scale of time. Wherever you go, into the past or into the future, you will find nothing but the present there. This is because thoughts of the past or the future are occurring in the timeless present. You can never escape the present. Even if you bring the past or the future into your awareness, you are doing so while you are in the present. Isn't it amazing?

If you visit the future, you will observe it while remaining in the experience of the present. You will realize without complaining, fearing or fantasizing, that the future is taking shape based on your present tendencies and patterns. The decisions you tend to take in various situations, the things you do when you encounter sorrow, the things you do when you get extra money, the things you do when you get spare time, the things you do when you are praised by people, the things you do when you get angry, etc. are shaping your future. The future is not something that will happen out of the blue. The future is not unpredictable. You will get the wisdom of what needs to be changed right now if you want a better future.

Similarly, when you visit the past while remaining in the space of the present, you get to learn valuable lessons. Instead of getting sucked in by past memories, you simply observe how your past behavior has shaped your present. By not drifting into feelings evoked by recalling the past, you remain in the space of the present. This is how the present is the space that transcends the scale of time. In this space, wherever you go, you find yourself in the present.

When the comparing, judging and vacillating mind is dropped, we enter the space of the present. We abide in pure consciousness. We allow all our decisions to be taken from the source of love, joy and peace. We don't allow our mind to interfere in this process. We simply flow along blissfully.

People find it difficult to surrender their mind because they think that it will help solve problems. When problems arise, people keep thinking of them again and again. Why? Because they think they will somehow be able to find solutions through thinking. But the law of nature is that whatever you focus on increases in life. If you focus on problems, problems get magnified. If you focus on solutions instead, you will find one. And solutions are an attribute of the space of the present. Only when you remain in the space of the present can you find solutions.

5

Dissolving Problems

Everyone has problems. Problems are part and parcel of life. How to tackle problems is the question that is the most discussed in self-help circles. Umpteen ways to deal with and overcome problems have been put forth so far. "Have a positive attitude," "Study the problem," "Define the problem in words," "Make a plan to overcome it," "Evaluate the results and redesign your plan," "Brainstorm the problem," "Talk to experts," "Stay cool and be brave," so on and so forth. You often hear these and more suggestions when you seek help in solving your problems. These are the half-secret that can help in overcoming your problems in life.

> **Half-secret**
>
> Focus on the problem, define it, brainstorm and plan to solve the problem.

But it can be overwhelming when you are stuck with a problem and you cannot budge unless the problem goes away. Personal problems, relationship problems, marital problems, money problems, legal problems, property disputes, problems at the workplace, are what most people come across on a regular basis. The only thing you see in life in such situations is the problem in front of you. It stands like a huge giant and takes up your entire field of vision, leaving you nothing else to see.

The secret – the full secret – reveals the knowledge that whatever you focus on increases in your life. If your problems seem huge, it is because they have fed on your focus to inflate to such a size. The food that your problems ingest is your wrong focus. The more you focus on problems in the wrong way, the bigger they grow in size.

Instead of wasting time, attention, thoughts and energy overtly on problems, it really helps to focus on what you really want in life. This is because when you focus on problems, it is with the feeling that you don't want them. You resist them.

Man lives in the illusion that he can prevent any situation from affecting him by resisting it. On the contrary, he is only increasing his woes by resisting his life situations. When you resist any situation, you give attention to it. The situation worsens as you energize it through your resistance. What you resist persists. Acceptance dissolves the resistance to whatever is.

Is accepting the situation practical? It may not sound workable. Yet, the proof of the pudding is in the eating. We can't realize the power of acceptance until we have tried it and experienced it for ourselves.

Accept and Allow Solutions to Emerge from Within

Situations are facts. We get caught up in them by mentally labeling them as 'problems'. Seeing any situation as a 'problem' is the real problem! Situations are the way they are, whether you agree or not. Resisting the fact of the situation results in fear, sorrow and frustration. Resistance destroys your ability to solve problems and tends to worsen the situation.

When you are resisting a situation, your mind is not open to all the possible options that exist. For the troubled and unclear mind, options seem to be limited. The state of such a mind is like driving the vehicle of life with a hazy windscreen. Common sense demands that you must wipe the windscreen clean so that your journey of life is safe. Accepting the problem situation helps clear the windscreen of the vehicle of life.

You may wonder whether you can achieve what you want if you keep submitting to everyday situations. Acceptance is not about being submissive or passive to the happenings of the world. It leads you to a space where the mind opens up to all the possible options for a solution. It does not mean you're in denial or running away from your problems.

The problem does not remain as-is when you accept it. By letting go and accepting the situation, you will find that you are able to see more clearly. When your vision is not clouded and you are able to see clearly, the problem no longer remains a problem. You begin to witness the beliefs and notions that are distorting your view, causing you to see it as a problem.

You give a chance for solutions to emerge from within you. You tap into the creative potential within and discover solutions that you could never have seen before. The solution is revealed to you intuitively.

When you resist a problem, you're actually blocking this marvelous process from working for you. Accepting the situation and allowing solutions to intuitively emerge is the only true way of addressing problems. By being in a frame of acceptance, you need not solve problems. Rather, you will witness solutions arising from the problem situation itself.

Focus on What You Really Want

Further to accepting and allowing, we need to train our focus on what we really want in life. We need to be focused on love, joy, happiness, peace, health and prosperity instead of focusing on the lack of it. Whatever we focus on increases.

> **Full-secret**
>
> Focus on what you really want. What you ultimately want is Love, Joy and Peace, rather than the means that lead to them. Solutions are bound to follow.

But will the change of focus make the problem go away? Won't the problem still remain? The answer is: when you shift your focus away from your problem, it will reduce to its original size, which is always smaller than your capabilities can handle. No problem in life can be any larger than the ambit of your capabilities.

Even before a problem arrives in your life, God first gives you the capability to overcome it. God never sends a problem in your life without first empowering you with the capability to solve it. This is His *Leela,* the divine game of life. We are here to discover and revel in this wondrous game called life!

Understanding the laws of nature opens up a whole new dimension to life. The law of focus is one such remarkable law that will help you overcome problems as easily as sliding a hot knife through butter. Let us understand the law of focus and how to wield the tool of focus to attain all that you want in life.

Now let us perform a little experiment. After reading this paragraph, close your eyes and do this exercise. With eyes closed for a minute or two, do NOT try to imagine a green monkey. Keep telling yourself every few seconds, "Do not visualize a green monkey." Start.

Now open your eyes. What happened? You did visualize the monkey, didn't you? Even when you were instructed not to, you did. In your mind's eye, you saw exactly what you were asked NOT to think about. What could be the reason for this? This happened because you had passed such an instruction through your thoughts and words to your subconscious mind. Our subconscious mind does not understand the words 'no' or 'not' as it cannot picture these words. Since the words 'no' and 'not' do not create any images, the opposite becomes true.

Think of the people who like to watch crime serials on TV. They often mutter, "If this had happened to me, I would have done this… I would have done that…" or "I hope this situation does not occur in my life," etc. Little do they realize that their focus is completely consumed by the crime they are watching. It would be no surprise if similar incidents do take place in such people's lives, even though they did NOT want them to happen.

Thus you can imagine how the law of focus works in our lives. Our feelings, thoughts, words and actions work like prayer. In fact, these are the real prayers you do in daily life. And whether you know it or not, each of our prayers is constantly being fulfilled. Your feelings and thoughts are more powerful than you can imagine. The vibrations that your state of mind produces attract similar things in life. Our abilities, our health, our success or failure, the people coming into our life, our financial condition, the incidents happening in our life, and our creativity are all created in our mind first. Only then do they manifest in visible form.

Each one of our thoughts and feelings creates their own unique vibration. The thing that resonates with this vibration gets attracted to us. If your thoughts create vibrations that match with prosperity, prosperity comes into your life. If your thoughts create vibrations that match with peace, peace comes into your life. If you create vibrations of love and health, you receive the wealth of love and health. Similarly, the opposite is also true. If you create vibrations of despair, hopelessness, sadness, anger, irritation, frustration, jealousy, hatred, and so on, you attract more and more of the same.

Anything that matches your vibration not just enters your life but also grows many times. The easiest way to benefit from this law of nature is to harness the power of focus positively – by employing it to achieve what you really want instead of what you don't want. Focus on what you want, and your vibration will match with it. The power of focus will direct all your mental energy towards it, and it will start growing at a steady pace.

This is just like watering a plant. The plant that you water grows at a steady pace while the plant that you neglect withers away. Everything needs energy to grow, and by focusing on the thing you want, you provide it with the energy of your attention.

Check where you are spending your valuable mental energy. Are you investing it in what you want by focusing on what you want? Or are you investing it in things that you don't want? Remember that you will receive the thing you focus on – whether it is positive or negative, desirable or undesirable. You will not only receive it but also multiply it several times.

The Action Plan

Now sit back and contemplate on what you really want – in personal life, in your family, at your workplace, in your relationships with people, in society, and so on. Make key decisions about how you intend to progress in various facets of life, about the kind of life you would love to lead.

It is very important to write down what you truly want in life. Otherwise, it all remains a fantasy only in our minds. When we note down the details about what we plan to do, about what our deepest intentions are, and why we would like to live the way we wish to, we will begin to experience a newfound peace and clarity.

Putting down our thoughts on paper helps us empty the unnecessary mental clutter and create space for new ideas and new possibilities to emerge. Write down your findings in your personal diary. Here are some examples that may help you in your contemplation:

- I want to have a platform of joyous communication and peaceful coexistence in my relationships, so that I can experience love, joy and peace in the family.

- I want simplicity and smoothness at work, so that everyone can be happy and healthy.

- I wish progress for myself and my colleagues, so that together we move to a higher level of consciousness with love, joy and peace.

- I want new, creative and challenging work, so that out of love, I can explore not just my highest potential, but that of others as well.

- I want a good salary, promotion and cooperation of my colleagues at work, so that I can handle all my responsibilities effectively and assist in the progress of the organization out of love, joy and peace.

- I wish for the betterment of everyone's physical, mental and financial conditions, so that our society can be loving, happy, peaceful and prosperous.

- I want peaceful coexistence in the world, so that everyone can experience love and joy.

With the help of the examples given above, make a list of what you want in each facet of your life, and link it to either love or joy or peace, or a combination of these attributes. From time to time, read this list and repeat the affirmations to yourself.

A whole new revolution can be brought about in the world merely by shifting focus. You will stop viewing problems as 'problems'; for you, they will be challenges that are meant to be relished. We are not born on earth to be consumed by problems. We are meant to play the game of overcoming obstacles and use them as a ladder to develop our core qualities and reach the highest state of consciousness; a state full of true love, joy and peace!

6

Beyond Personality and Character

The manager of a company once conducted a job interview. He found one candidate very intelligent, energetic, and passionate about his career. As the interview progressed, the manager became more and more impressed with the candidate's confidence, way of speaking and body language. He thought he had found the perfect person for the job. But at the last moment, he spotted an anomaly in the candidate's resume. Upon probing further, it became clear that the candidate had lied at one place in his resume.

The manager had almost made up his mind to hire him. He was very impressed with his personality. But the flaw in the candidate's character made him change his mind. He chose to hire another candidate whose personality was not all that impressive but seemed to have a solid base of character. This candidate was not very expressive. He spoke in a mellowed voice, and was not trying hard to impress the manager. But he was not a job hopper, he politely but firmly expressed his expectations, and asked the manager what else he would like to know about him. He answered each question correctly and even gave multiple solutions for each problem asked.

This story elucidates the difference between personality and character. People can be introverted or extroverted, shy or confident, serious or funny, laid back or highly energetic, calm or talkative, and so on. All these are nothing but personality traits. Personality can be easily to read. If not during the first interaction, a few more interactions are enough to get to know someone's personality.

Half-secret

> Looking good is important in life. Develop your personality appeal to succeed.
>
> Complete character = Top Ten + Inner Ninety.

Character, on the other hand, is something much deeper. Character stands on the pillars of principles. It takes far longer to get to know someone's character. Character traits reveal themselves only in specific and often uncommon circumstances. Honesty, trustworthiness, maturity, integrity, sincerity, purpose of life, selflessness, empathy, true love, are some such traits.

The half-secret is that personality contributes only 10% to our success while character contributes 90%. Personality is visible while character is not easily visible. This is just like the structure of a building. A building's foundation is not visible to the eye, but it provides 90% of the stability that a building needs for standing tall. If a building is constructed without a foundation, a minor earthquake or a strong gush of wind is enough to topple it over. The part of the building that is visible contributes hardly 10% to its own stability. In the same way, a person's overall existence is made 90% of character and 10% of personality.

For the sake of emphasizing their meaning and importance, let us refer to the character as the 'Inner Ninety' and the personality as the 'Top Ten'. A person's appearance, mannerisms, nature, facial expressions, body language, style quotient and lifestyle are all part of the Top Ten. And his temperament, thinking, habits and qualities are part of the Inner Ninety. The Inner Ninety needs to be deep and strong if you want to march ahead towards true progress and success in life. A good Top Ten may help in attaining success, but it requires a strong Inner Ninety to sustain success.

Top Ten is no doubt important to a certain extent. You need to take care of your body, improve your health, keep yourself physically and mentally fit, improve your power of communication, improve body language, learn to express yourself clearly, and so on. But far more important than taking care of Top Ten is the need to take care of Inner Ninety. If you improve your Inner Ninety, your Top Ten will automatically improve. You won't have to take extra efforts for it. The stronger the Inner Ninety, the better will Top Ten work. Without a strong Inner Ninety, the Top Ten cannot sustain for long.

> Two neighbors, Nikhil and Anil, went to buy new cars for themselves. As soon as Nikhil saw a dazzling car with attractive

color and design, he fell in love with it and immediately bought it. Anil, on the other hand, compared the details of each car, made an in-depth study of the features. After taking test-drives of several cars, he finally bought an ordinary-looking car. Nikhil laughed at Anil's decision in his mind and felt proud of his own choice. Even Anil's family was a bit displeased and they liked Nikhil's car better. But Anil was confident of his choice. A month later, Nikhil's pride turned to envy. His car's fuel economy was poor and maneuvering the car through traffic was difficult. Anil's ordinary-looking car, on the other hand, was a pleasure in every aspect. Anil and his family were extremely pleased with their car's performance.

Now, there is a question for you. If you were in their place, which car would you choose? The car with an attractive Top Ten but poor Inner Ninety, or the car with an ordinary Top Ten but great Inner Ninety? Common sense suggests that we should buy the latter, because now you have the full view of both cars. But unfortunately, most of us don't take a full view of things in life. We remain fixated with the attractive Top Ten.

The primary reason for this is that the media keeps focusing on the Top Ten. Advertisements, interviews, movies and television shows constantly focus on looks, clothes, makeup, jewelry, gadgets, and luxurious goods. They impress upon us how to shine our outer personality so as to attract people's attention. No advertisement explores the hidden foundation in us. Nobody asks us to strengthen our Inner Ninety through prayer, contemplation and focus.

It is true that Top Ten has its own importance, because it creates the first impression. But if someone is hollow from within, it takes no time for this impression to fall. On the other hand, there have been many living examples of people with very ordinary Top Ten but extraordinary Inner Ninety. There is perhaps no better example than Helen Keller. In spite of being blind and deaf since infancy, she earned a Bachelor of Arts degree, became a political activist and authored several popular books.

There have also been many movie actors in the world, who had an impressive outer personality. They had legions of fans and were simply adored by people. They achieved great heights in their respective careers. But yet, they lived a sad, depressed and tumultuous life. In spite of having all the luxuries of the world, they had no wealth of character.

So the secret, rather the half-secret, can be summed up as:

Complete character = Top Ten + Inner Ninety

Hidden Infinity - The Essence of Who-We-Truly-Are

In the competitive world, personality is often used as a mask to flaunt who we are as individuals. But personality is actually a superficial outfit. Make-up of the personality doesn't cause any harm unless we believe that we *are* the personality. It is not difficult to notice that no matter how much we may beautify our personality, we still lack the fulfillment of who-we-truly-are. True fulfillment is experienced when we dwell in the essence of who-we-truly-are.

Full-secret

> Being who you truly are is the purpose of life. Wake-up to who-you-truly-are through inner make-up.
>
> Ideal life = Top Ten + Inner Ninety + Hidden Infinity

This third entity is the most important element that makes a human being complete… this element is the Creator and Enlivening entity of human life… it is what drives us to experience and express ourselves in the world. Without this third entity, human life cannot exist. Why is this entity called as 'Hidden Infinity'? Why is it 'hidden' and why is it 'infinity'? It is 'hidden' because it can neither be seen with the eyes, nor imagined with the mind, nor understood with the intellect. It is called 'Infinity' because it permeates the whole universe and cannot be measured. It has no form, shape, color or scale. It is not like the Top Ten or Inner Ninety that can be measured or evaluated. Self-realized masters, who have transcended the limited personality and character, have reveled in the experience of this Hidden Infinity and given it different names like God, Consciousness, Source, Self, and so on.

Each of us is brimming with this Hidden Infinity. It is the very essence of who-we-truly-are. It is the core of our being. To know this Hidden Infinity is to know our true self. And this is what is known as Self-realization.

Without experiencing the Hidden Infinity, there can be no satisfaction in human life. Your highest possibilities as a human being can be unlocked only when you experience the Hidden Infinity. Due to ignorance of their highest possibilities, most people on earth live a very ordinary and meaningless life, and depart without attaining the highest fulfillment and completeness.

The experience of the Hidden Infinity opens up life's highest possibilities. When you know the Hidden Infinity, it is like discovering the instruction manual of your body and life. And this knowing already exists within each of us! It is just that we are not directly aware of its presence. It is life itself, and it is the same for every human being on earth. True spirituality helps you gain the whole understanding of this Hidden Infinity.

Many people believe that spirituality is only meant for old, depressed or worried people. Such misconceptions need to be removed. Experiencing the Hidden Infinity is top priority for each and every human being. In fact, it is beyond all the priorities! It is only after experiencing it that you can truly get to know yourself. And it is only after getting to know yourself that you can blossom and express yourself at your highest potential.

So the full-secret can be summed up as:

Ideal life = Top Ten + Inner Ninety + Hidden Infinity

In the increasingly fast world today, most people lead lives of quiet desperation. They go through the rigors of life never realizing the full beauty of all that life has to offer. Most people simply exist, rather than engage in life fully. The primary reason for this is that they neglect the spiritual aspect of their existence. They only focus on the body and mind. Think about it. We are living longer lives than ever before. We have developed technology that enables us to do things that were just impossible a few years ago. Most of us are more prosperous than our forefathers. Yet, the quality of life in terms of happiness, contentment and completeness seems to elude us.

In spite of great success, the high-flying businessman with a dream life still feels something lacking in life. The successful doctor that gives a new lease of life to hundreds of patients still feels a void. When Alexander the Great was asked what he would do after conquering the world, he went into depression. He sensed a great void and didn't know how to fill it. What does all this point to? It only points to lack of fulfilling the spiritual dimension of our existence. This desire needs to be addressed with top priority.

Everyone has a need to feel connected to a higher source. Everyone also needs to feel that life has purpose and meaning. This is what Hidden Infinity is all about! When you raise your consciousness to understand our unity with God and all of life, these needs will be fulfilled. Attaining Hidden Infinity is attaining the active power of God. This active power is the same power that breathes life into this universe – right from the smallest of creatures deep inside the ocean to the mighty constellation of galaxies.

After you get to know Hidden Infinity, it will be clear to you that your body is nothing but a means to express Hidden Infinity. You will realize that you need to empty your body of vices and tendencies, so that it becomes like a temple of God – clean, mighty, pure and pious. This is for allowing God (Hidden Infinity) to work in the best possible way through your body.

Most people keep decorating their personalities and enriching their characters without knowing who they truly are. They are lost to their real essence. They spend time and energy in the make-up of their bodies and personalities. If you embellish yourself so as to gratify your ego, then such make-up cannot give lasting fulfillment.

When you invest your attention in the idea of an individual persona, you keep moving away from your true nature. By decorating the personality, you promote the individual ego.

However, when you use make-up after realizing your true identity, for expressing the Hidden Infinity, then the motivation is to wake-up in the make-up. When you rise above individuality and gain conviction in your true nature as pure consciousness, you will live with the intention: "My body is a temple. When people look at my Top Ten, it should raise their consciousness. They should develop faith in leading a life by knowing their true nature." Make-up done with this understanding is invaluable.

Your appearance should be presentable to people, and they should be inspired to follow the path of Truth when they look up to you. Then the Top Ten and Inner Ninety will truly serve the Hidden Infinity, bringing lasting peace and joy.

When humans strive to strengthen their Inner Ninety and seek to experience the Hidden Infinity at the same time, they achieve true success. Their purpose on earth is fulfilled!

7

The Ultimate Goal of Life

No matter how successful we are in our professional life, no matter how many friends we have, no matter how prosperous our family is, and no matter how loving our relationships are, we always yearn for 'something else' to give a sense of completion to our quests as human beings.

Knowingly or unknowingly, we are always on the lookout for a deep and everlasting sense of bliss and love. Nothing that we achieve in the external world seems to be capable of filling up the void that we feel inside. At some point of time, every human being turns inward in the hope of finding fulfillment within himself. And thus begins the journey of Self-realization.

> **Half-secret**
>
> Self-realization – experiencing your true Self – is the ultimate goal of life.

As human beings, we have a body-mind mechanism provided to us. All of us try to fulfill the wishes of this body-mind mechanism to feel satisfied. But there is a limit to which satisfaction can be felt by pampering the body-mind. This is because we are not the body-mind mechanism. We are its users and the body-mind is our tool. We are the driver of this mechanism. Unless we do not fulfill the ultimate wish of who-we-truly-are, the ultimate contentment, fulfillment, love, joy and bliss cannot be experienced.

The Purpose of Life

When people are not prepared to receive higher answers, they are told, "The goal of life is to become a doctor, or an engineer, or just to be successful. If you want to become a carpenter, then become a good carpenter. If you aspire to become a doctor, become a good doctor."

Initially, such answers seem adequate. However, it is only when one is prepared to receive higher understanding that they get higher answers: The goal of human life is that 'life should know life'. Life, in this context, refers to the inner experience of aliveness within each one of us, which has been known as Self or God. It is the living consciousness due to which the body is alive and moving. In the absence of the enlivening consciousness, the body would be a mere corpse. The body moves only because of the presence of the Self, the conscious presence.

Let life return unto itself; let life experience its own essence. When the living principle in a body is consciously aware of itself, it is called Self-realization. Self here refers to God or Consciousness, the Source of everything, the very essence of life itself. 'The goal of life is life itself' means that the purpose of human life is to be in the experience of the Self.

Self-realization is the recognition of who we truly are. Once we discover our true self, our ultimate quest as human beings comes to an end. Until then, we keep indulging in bodily, mental, intellectual and egoistic pleasures. If we feel disturbed, distressed or sad, we simply seek solace in friends, television, music, food, drinks, etc. This is like digging a second pit to fill soil into the first pit. For some time, the disturbance goes away. But very soon the void of the second pit starts disturbing us. To fill the void we dig a third pit, and so on. The emptiness simply shifts from here to there; it never goes away. Most people waste an entire lifetime digging new pits to fill old ones.

The real need is to satiate our emptiness once and for all by getting to know our true self. Our true self is the oneness that fills creation. This oneness is what we call as God, the universal consciousness, highest awareness, ultimate bliss, and so on. Our true self is the source of life. It is the essence of our greatest possibility. It is an unending source of energy, enthusiasm, love, joy and peace. When we tap into this unending source, the ultimate contentment is experienced.

Self-realization is a state of liberation from the sense of separateness and merger into oneness. This sense of separateness is the cause of all misery in life – fear, anxiety, worry, anger, depression, sadness, etc. With Self-realization, all misery comes to an end. All bondages that tie us down in this world snap. Just imagine; once we come to know that we are the oneness behind everything, what fear can remain? What anxiety, worry or sadness can remain? Such negative feelings are associated only with the sense of separateness. If we are not separate, there can be nothing to worry about.

It is only in order to realize who-you-truly-are and express its divine qualities that you have been associated with your body. When you know the real meaning of life, you will also understand the art of 'being life'. Many people wish to learn the art of living. But we don't have to learn the art of living; we need to learn the art of *being* life itself. This means that we have to shift our focus from the objects of perception to that which enables perception, from thought to that which enables thinking. We will then rise above the changing and limited to that which is changeless, eternal, and boundless.

Before Self-realization, you lead life assuming yourself to be a body. You identify yourself with your body and often say, "This person appreciated me; that person made fun of me..." However, all this happens not with you, but with your body-mind mechanism.

Whatever we pursue in our lives is the foreground. Self-realization is the background of all pursuits. When you are unaware of this whole-and-sole life purpose, you don't work at it. But when you gain clarity, you won't miss a single opportunity that helps you to progress further toward Self-realization.

Is There Anything Beyond Self-Realization?

What can be the full secret about Self-realization? Is there anything beyond Self-realization? The answer is yes, because Self-realization is only the beginning! The ultimate goal of life is to stabilize (be established) in the state of Self-realization and then express the divine qualities of the Self.

There are many who experience momentary flashes of oneness when they are in the midst of pure nature or even in their daily lives. However, these are only samples of the experience of Self-realization, mere glimpses that happen when the understanding of our true nature shines forth.

Such glimpses are experienced when the judgmental mind momentarily becomes silent. But what happens after the glimpse? The judgmental mind emerges again and takes credit for the experience: "I performed meditation; I attained this deeply profound state; I experienced Self-realization." The mind lacks the understanding that it cannot experience the Self.

The mind takes up the task of realizing the Self, as if it were possible for the mind to do so. However, the obstinate mind that 'tries' to realize the Self is actually a hurdle. When this mind is stilled, the Self experiences itself. This is the full-secret. Self-stabilization happens when the comparing and judging aspect of the mind drops and no longer emerges. It is about permanently and constantly abiding in the experience of pure consciousness. One lives with the firm conviction of one's true nature beyond the body and mind.

Self-realization without understanding is futile. It is meaningless to proclaim that you have attained Self-realization based on a one-time experience, without being permanently stabilized in that experience. There are many self-proclaimed masters who claim that they have attained Self-realization. Their ego is boosted and they consequently indulge in gaining credit and recognition that gratify their ego.

> ### Full-secret
> Self-realization is a one-time glimpse of the Truth. The ultimate goal is Self-stabilization – being established permanently in the experience of Self, followed by Self-expression –expressing the divine qualities of Self.

Self-stabilization is the ultimate purpose of life. If the body continues to indulge in old tendencies and habits even after many such glimpses of the Self, then the ultimate purpose is not served. The judgmental mind keeps returning with false beliefs and doubts about the experience of the Self. Due to this interference of the judging mind, the state of inner stillness in which the Self experiences itself remains veiled.

With Self-stabilization comes Self-expression – the expression of the Self through the body-mind mechanism. On attaining Self-stabilization at the age of thirty-five, the Buddha continued to spread the message of Truth till the ripe age of eighty. Siddhartha Gautama's body served as a medium for expression of the Buddha, the Self.

When the purpose of Self-stabilization is not clear, you might assume glimpses on the path as Self-realization and mistake that to be the ultimate goal. If Self-realization is seen as Self-stabilization, then that is the ultimate goal. If you see it as a one-time experience, then it is just the beginning.

IMPORTANCE OF TRAINING THE BODY-MIND MECHANISM

Glimpses of the Self can come about either as the feeling of oneness with all creation or as the nothingness beyond thoughts. These glimpses do come in various situations. One can also access this state (popularly known as an altered state of consciousness, or being in the 'zone') through various rituals such as regulated breathing or even in adventure vehicles. The mind goes blank and the stillness behind the mind is experienced.

However, when the mind returns, it memorizes such glimpses. Self-realization is then wrongly believed to be an event that happened in the past. However, the question to be asked to this mind is: Is it a living experience right now? If it is not being experienced in the present, then it was just a glimpse that has faded away; it is just a figment of memory.

As the credit-taking mind doesn't realize this, it assumes, "I have achieved the ultimate state." This can lead to a dangerous turn in life. Such a person may start propagating his half-wisdom and cause damage to society.

Any claim by anyone that links Self-realization to a one-time epiphany or satori or a supernatural event does not hold. Self-realization is the most ordinary state that is experienced as the constant presence of Self-awareness, because it is essentially who-you-truly-are.

With Self-realization, there is every chance of backsliding, of falling back due to the entangling habits of the body-mind. If the body-mind mechanism where Self-realization has been experienced is still a victim of habits that entangle the Self, the glimpses of Self-realization have not served the real purpose.

Hence, while the glimpses of Self-experience do happen, it is essential to train the comparing, judging, doubting, and blaming mind to be silent. The goal is to permanently get rid of thinking patterns, habits and tendencies that do not allow the Self to be self-aware. The purpose is to surrender the ego (the feeling of separateness) and stabilize in the experience of the Self. A true Guru can lead you to such a state. He imparts the right understanding of the Truth. He cautions you about potential risks on the way. He helps you train your mind to become still so that Self-experience is established within your body-mind.

Self-stabilization is also about raising your body-mind's capacity to hold the experience of Self-awareness. What happens if you pass a large amount of current through a low-wattage bulb? The bulb burns out. The bulb, in this case, represents the human body-mind and the current represents the Truth. When the understanding of the Truth dawns for the first time in a human body-mind, it can be called Self-realization. But to hold on to that Truth permanently without falling to tendencies and mind patterns, it is essential to raise the capacity of the body-mind.

The process of self-stabilization involves eradication of past conditioning with the guidance imparted by the Guru. The disciple performs constant contemplation even while going about his activities and encountering various incidents in life. Past programming reveals itself only during and after incidents. The disciple observes his own mind during activities and incidents. He reflects upon his thinking patterns. He meditates upon his Self constantly, even if he is in a busy marketplace. In the process, his mind gets cleansed of habits and tendencies.

What Happens After Self-Stabilization?

After Self-stabilization, what happens is not change, but transformation. Change is just an alteration; transformation is a paradigm shift. For example, when you begin to climb the stairs to reach the terrace, you move from the first step to the second. Though this is a change, you are still on the stairs. When you move from the second step to the third, you can probably get a better view of the terrace, but you continue to be on the stairs. This is 'change'. When you move beyond the stairs onto the terrace, this is called a shift or 'transformation'.

With change, ignorance continues, because you still perceive from the level of the mind through judgments, logical premise, assumptions and memory. However, with transformation, the entire structure of the programmed mind is transcended. You rise above the stairs of mental perceptions and intuitively know from the terrace of the Self.

Suppose you are sitting in a room where there are pillars that block your view of the entire room. You keep changing your position in the room, so as to get a better view. However, you still cannot see the room in its entirety as the pillars obstruct a complete one-time view. But when you get into a helicopter that hovers above the room, you get a complete simultaneous view of everything as it is. You are also able to see what the others in the room are not able to see and which pillars are blocking their view.

In the same way, before Self-stabilization, you keep refining your perspective of life by going around the pillars of beliefs that block the experience of reality. However, rising beyond all beliefs, the mind is transcended; the all-encompassing reality is intuitively known by the Self. This is transformation.

After Self-stabilization, one transcends the opposites of happiness and sorrow, attachment and aversion, praise and censure, life and death. For example, it is a common belief that the Self-realized one becomes mild or humble. 'Becoming humble' presupposes the existence of a separate individual who has to 'become' humble. However, stabilizing in the Self leads to transcendence of both—ego and humility. There is liberation, not only from sorrow, but also from happiness. The individual who says 'I have attained Self-realization' no longer exists.

With Self-stabilization follows Self-expression – the expression of divine qualities of the Self, such as love, joy, peace, compassion, patience, consistency to name a few. The pure presence begins to stir the Self within other bodies to awaken and realize the Truth. The very presence of one who is established in the Self is a healing presence, radiating love and joy to everyone around.

8

You are Meditation

You would have heard the story of Aladdin and the genie that keeps tormenting him, asking him for more work. Aladdin's genie is constantly at his service. He can't remain idle even for a minute. Furthermore, the genie warns Aladdin that if he doesn't give him something to do, he will finish Aladdin. Aladdin constantly assigns him some work or the other, but the genie completes it in no time. Aladdin is fast running out of ideas and losing sleep. Who will now free Aladdin from this relentless genie?

The human mind is no different from this genie. It finds it difficult to remain idle even for a minute. It constantly seeks some activity or the other. As a result, we end up giving it something to do, something to think, quite often what we don't really need it to do. The mind is uncomfortable with boredom. When it is bored and idle, it can meander into the past, or mull about the future.

In many cases, the mind uses idle time to engage in blame and criticism, getting into needless arguments, and so on. The mind can even put up with negative things, just for the sake of avoiding idleness and boredom. Why else would it love to watch tragedies or violent movies!

We may perhaps not realize, but a restless mind can drain all our energy. We find ourselves stressed and agitated when the mind throws its tantrums. Another trait of the mind is of bouncing back. The more we try to control it, the more it rebels and persists with its whims. And the more we give into its whims, the more it holds sway.

As our creative energy is dissipated in the ceaseless chatter of the mind, we may find it difficult to focus in the present and act effectively. This can lead to loss of productivity – both efficiency and effectiveness. Since we are not able to meet our expectations, our anxiety and stress levels rise. This can also adversely affect our relationships at home and office.

In severe cases, people even tend to lose confidence, which can often lead to depression. Every time impurities such as boredom, ego, differentiation, fear, anger, greed, jealousy, or hatred, arise in the mind, life seems miserable. Eventually we are likely to wonder, "Is this a proper way to lead life – swinging between joy and sorrow, success and failure? Is it ever possible to lead a life that is happy, peaceful and harmonious? If so, how?"

The answer is: by quieting the mind. The mind is totally silent when we are in deep sleep. The moment we wake up in the morning, it becomes active again. Under normal circumstances, we can't coerce the mind to refrain from activity when it is hyperactive. The practice of meditation is the one thing that can help in quieting the mind whenever we choose.

THE PRACTICE OF MEDITATION TECHNIQUES

By practicing various techniques of meditation with the understanding of their gross and subtle aspects, it is possible for us to quiet the mind. With consistent practice of meditation, our mind becomes unshaken and disciplined. Instead of the mind becoming our master, *we* become the master of our mind. Like a sincere aide, our mind serves only when we really need it to; else it remains still.

> **Half-secret**
> Practice meditation using concentration techniques to focus and quiet the mind. Meditation is for calming the mind and becoming peaceful and productive.

Every technique of meditation begins with a preparatory stage. In this stage, we prepare our body for sitting still for a period of time. We wear appropriate clothing, we sit in a proper place and posture; we follow certain rituals with hand postures and chanting of words. We instruct our mind to be receptive during the meditation session.

In the next stage, we engage our mind on a chosen object in order to focus it in one direction. There are multitudes of techniques available like chanting, visualizing, listening, sensing, etc.

The purpose of these techniques is to focus the mind on one point to the exclusion of everything else. This enhances the effectiveness and focus of the mind.

There are also practices like mindfulness and *Vipassana*, which focus on raising awareness about whatever is happening in the present moment. These attention techniques focus on observing all sensations, movements, emotions and happenings in a detached manner.

These techniques provide various benefits. They help in raising our productivity and capacity. Our mind becomes tranquil. The body becomes disciplined through the practice of consistency and persistence. Needless to say, these benefits, in turn, can bring good health, harmony, and career growth.

The Essence of Meditation – Beyond Techniques

The understanding that meditation is a technique meant to focus and silence the mind is the half-secret.

There are various misconceptions regarding the meaning of meditation. The word 'meditation' has so many different connotations. As the words attention, contemplation, and meditation are used interchangeably, the word 'meditation' has lost its deeper significance.

For example, the phrase 'to meditate upon' has almost the same connotation as 'to contemplate upon'. When you say, "I am meditating upon the next course of action," you are actually contemplating. You are dealing with the content of thoughts. To meditate upon or to contemplate signifies looking at a topic from all aspects or to get into the depth of a topic. But true meditation is very different from 'meditating upon'.

When you say, "I am meditating on a candle-flame," this is merely concentration. It is about focusing your attention on a single object. Most people focus on techniques pertaining to the body and mind, only to attain a high degree of concentration. However, this is far from the essence of meditation. Contemplation and concentration are merely tools to enter the state of meditation.

Chanting (*naam-smaran*), focusing on breath, listening to sounds, observing thoughts, mantras, etc. are also part of the second stage. True meditation is the third stage – the state of being.

Meditation is the essence of who-you-truly-are; it is not a tool. When you use tools such as contemplation, concentration, chanting, observing, listening, etc. your mind becomes steady. Once your mind becomes steady and focused, you become ready to enter the state of real meditation.

There are many who practice mindfulness – the practice of observing whatever is happening at the physical and mental planes. They observe every action, every movement and consider that as meditation. Again, mindfulness has its benefits in terms of calming the mind. However, mindfulness is not meditation.

Now let us understand what meditation truly is. Meditation is the nature of the real Self; it is your essential nature. You ARE meditation. Meditation is the state of the Self when it is absorbed in itself. It is when consciousness is conscious of itself.

Full-secret

> You are meditation. Realize that your conscious presence is meditation. Meditation is the state beyond doing and non-doing. It is a state of being absorbed in Self-awareness. Whether thoughts occur or not, it does not matter. The mind has no role to play in it.

In simple words, the practice of meditation means 'doing nothing.' However, some people find 'doing nothing' very difficult. They try to do 'nothing' instead of 'doing nothing.' Actually, mediation is beyond 'doing' and 'non-doing', because it is 'being'.

People question how it is possible to do 'nothing'. This is like asking, "What should I do to fall asleep?" You have to do nothing to fall asleep. You just need to lie down. If you try to bring sleep, sleep won't happen. It's an effortless process. Similarly, meditation is an effortless process in which you don't need to do anything; your very presence is meditation. You just allow meditation to happen by being available to it.

When we're caught up in the external world of relationships, wealth, status, or power, all our senses get completely engrossed in them. The practice of meditation liberates us from the attachments and aversions of the external world and directs us within, onto the experience of pure presence. All our senses, which are focused on the external world, are redirected within. The eye returns onto the eye. In other words, the eye feels or experiences itself; the ear returns onto the ear. All the senses feel and experience themselves. When the senses return onto themselves, it helps to delve deep within.

Liberation from the external world is not the real purpose. Defocusing from the external world is only a preparation for true meditation. Due to this missing link, meditation has been misconstrued as the practice of defocusing from the world. The original purpose of meditation techniques is to permanently abide in the Self. In order to refer to this original purpose without causing confusion, let us use a new term: Self-Meditation.

Self-Meditation means being established in the seat of pure awareness. In this state, the Knower becomes aware of the Knower through everything that is being known. It is like a double-headed arrow, while attention is directed to the world, it is also being directed to the source of attention. The experiencer experiences the experiencer through every experience. Every experience serves as a mirror to experience the knower, the subject.

Thus, the full-secret is that meditation is the ultimate state of Self-awareness that the various meditation techniques should lead to.

You are Already Thoughtless

During meditation, all kinds of thoughts arise. These thoughts torment us because we're attached and identified with them. When you get stuck with your thoughts, you identify yourself with them and think, "This is happening with me." Then you feel depressed.

But you do have an alternative. Thoughts can be witnessed as flares that arise in the sky of awareness. When you watch a thought from a distance, without focusing on its content, you can enjoy the wondrous display that arises in the sky of awareness. When you watch thoughts like flares in the sky, you remain untouched by them. They appear for some time and then fade away.

You can use thoughts as a double-headed arrow. While thoughts carry content and meaning, they also convey the fundamental news that you are alive. You, as awareness, can become aware of your own presence through the medium of thoughts that arise. Everything that happens is an opportunity to shift to the underlying truth – that all this is coming alive in the presence of the awareness.

This also brings to light yet another key missing link in the practice of meditation. Many seekers who practice meditation yearn to attain the thoughtless state. They long for the state of blankness where there are no thoughts. They try, in vain, to stop the flow of thoughts. In an attempt to resist thoughts, they only increase the thought current!

The full-secret is that there is no need to explicitly bring the thoughtless state. Your true nature is already thoughtless. It is pure awareness, devoid of thoughts. It is from this thoughtless state that thoughts arise. Whether thoughts arise or not, it does not matter to the real 'you' as you are already thoughtless from the very beginning.

The Risks of Being Stuck with Techniques

All techniques of meditation are merely preliminary steps to rein in the mind and prepare it for the ultimate purpose. When people get bogged down in these techniques without the right understanding of the real purpose, various distractions can spring up in the way.

For example, many people report getting various creative ideas regarding diverse subjects while preparing the mind for meditation. Improved powers of concentration and awareness lead to the generation of various creative ideas. If you get caught up in these, you lose out on true meditation. While these ideas may be brilliant and may help you greatly in your work, this was not the purpose with which you started.

Nothing can be more brilliant than meeting your true Self – the supreme consciousness which is the Source of everything. If at all you want to make use of these creative ideas, you can set aside a separate session for them. Don't mix meditation with creative ideas.

On the path of meditation, one also reaps immense rewards in physical, financial, professional, as well as social life. Consider these as a bonus, rather than getting entangled in them. These gains are not your goal. The real goal is Self-realization, after which nothing else can be more attractive to you.

In conclusion, true meditation is 'awareness of the Self'. It cannot be a tool or means. It cannot be *done*, for you can only *be* that. The mind has no role to play in it. It is not a path; it is the destination. And stabilizing in the state of meditation is the whole and sole purpose of human life.

9

Desires – To Have or Not to Have

Why do we suffer in life? What exactly is the cause of sorrow? These are age-old questions that every earnest seeker of Truth has pondered.

However, when answers are not easily forthcoming, what do most people do? Instead of delving deeper within to find answers, they perhaps let them pass by without giving them a second thought. They prefer to hide these questions below the carpet of material comforts. They find it easier to lose themselves in the distractions around and rest in the old comfort zone of ignorance.

Let us look deeper at the real cause of suffering. Suppose you expect your friend to appreciate you, and he surprisingly criticizes you for some reason. You feel dejected.

At the surface, it may appear that your friend's critical comments are the cause of your sorrow. But if you look deeper, you find that the sorrow was not because of his comments, but rather because your desire for appreciation was thwarted by him. When a desire is not fulfilled, it seems to cause sorrow.

But is that all? Is non-fulfillment of desires the real cause of suffering? Or is it the existence of desires itself?

Desires are one of the most inevitable aspects of the human mind. No one can deny the fact that all of us have some desire or the other, if not several! They may be either long-term goals or short-term wants. We all experience the craving for something that we long for. We also experience the aversion for something that we despise. And this is where we become victims, because wanting something does not always guarantee fulfillment.

Half-secret
Desires are the root cause of suffering.

Since ancient times, desire has been considered as the root cause of suffering. Many religious texts and philosophies have spoken at length about how desires only lead to pain eventually, if not immediately.

Spiritual pursuits have hinged around putting an end to all forms of desires. It has been an oft-followed practice for spiritual seekers to renounce productive life and retire into seclusion away from worldly life. All this is to put an end to desires, so as to attain 'Enlightenment'.

However, having come into this world, does keeping away from it serve the purpose? Truth has to transcend both worldly life and the life of renunciation. Truth cannot be one-sided. It exists beyond both the ways of life. Hence, the solution to this quandary does not lie in escaping from worldly life. Considering desires as the cause of sorrow is the half-secret.

Changing the external life circumstances or lifestyle cannot cause lasting inner transformation. We have to look within at the root cause of suffering. And worldly existence – amidst relationships and challenges of material life – provides an effective testing platform to check whether we are learning and growing.

Desire, or the *Desirer*

If we look even deeper, we will find that desires are not the real cause of suffering. The real cause of suffering is the ignorance of the one who entertains desires – the *desirer*.

It is like saying that knives are a cause of pain. Why would knives cause pain! After all, a knife is only a man-made tool meant to serve a purpose. The cause of pain is the person who uses the knife. A knife can be used by a criminal, as well as by a surgeon. One has the intention of taking someone's life, while the other intends to save a life. While the knife in the hands of a criminal is a curse as it eventually leads him to sorrow, the same knife in a surgeon's hands can become a boon that helps him fulfill his purpose. Thus, a knife can cause pain if the user does not know how to use it.

What are desires? They are nothing but tools that help in manifesting our real purpose. They help in channeling our creative potential.

Desires are like double-edged swords. If a desire is fulfilled, it can strengthen the ego. Else, it can cause disappointment.

Full-secret

> The habit of entertaining desires is the root cause of suffering. Attachment to desires arising from identification with the desirer is the real cause of suffering.

We need to learn how to use this double-edged sword effectively without getting hurt. Then fulfillment of desire will not bloat the ego. The non-fulfillment of desire will not cause suffering. We can then entertain desires and also say, "Enough of trivial desires! Let us now have such a desire that no one on earth has ever entertained before." Such an auspicious desire can come only if we have gained clarity about how desires affect us.

ATTACHMENT AND THE HABIT OF DESIRING

Man gets attached to desires. This is akin to a person holding a knife by the blade instead of the handle. It is bound to cause pain.

If we do not know the technique of using desires, and do not have the knowledge of the ultimate truth of life, then desires can breed attachment. If desires are not fulfilled, they entangle us making it difficult to get out of them. When we are disappointed and depressed, there is a tendency to brooding.

Desires, by themselves, are not the cause of misery. It is attachment to desire that leads to endless seeking, craving or aversion, and frustration. Attachment implies a sense of obsession, infatuation or fixation. To be free from attachment is to be free from suffering.

Attachment to relationships, roles that we play at home or the workplace, titles, money, comforts and conveniences, lead to the tendency of acquisition and preservation. When we do not know our true nature, we constantly seek gratification in the external world. We remain engaged in acquiring what we lack and preserving what we fear we may lose. This tendency of acquisition and preservation is a vicious cycle of attachment that leads to sorrow.

Attachment or obsession occurs when we claim ownership of objects, relationships, comforts, etc. When we mentally lay aside our claims, knowing that these objects and relationships are impermanent and have no bearing whatsoever on our internal state of happiness, we will no longer be attached to desires.

Does this mean that we lose our love and passion for life and its affairs? Not at all! The passion will still be there, and yet, it will be a detached passion.

There is nothing wrong with entertaining desires, as long as we are not victim to the habit of desiring. This is a subtle thing. We may desire worldly comforts and pursue them, until we find that they do not give lasting happiness. We then go after spiritual pursuits. What happens there? The habit of desiring is still going on. Earlier we may have desired material objects; but now we chase spiritual imaginations.

We cannot free ourselves by letting go of our attachment to any particular object or person, because it is then replaced by something or someone that we consider 'better'. In other words, we cannot give up anything, unless we hold onto something that seems 'better' to us. And then we get attached to the 'better' thing!

Letting Go of the *Desirer* – The One Who is Attached

We can attain true freedom from all sorrow only when we let go of the one who is attached – the separate individual that we assume ourselves to be. When we cling to the idea of being a unique individual, separate from totality, we experience fear, sorrow and anger. From attachment springs the fear that your desire may not be fulfilled, sorrow when the desire does not bear fruit, and anger with whatever seems to obstruct it.

The solution lies in steering clear from thoughts that are based on the limited 'I', 'me', and 'mine'. Insulate yourself from the grip of the limited personality through the practice of detachment. You need to first rise above these thoughts and see them for what they truly are. Then you can derive joy by partaking of worldly pleasures, without being attached to them.

At a fundamental level, it's about detachment from thoughts. The content of your thoughts shapes your beliefs. True detachment is about giving up the affinity for the content of thoughts. It's about being in a state of indifference to the content of thoughts.

We should receive everything that comes to us in the wrapper of detachment. With this understanding our prayer will change, "O God! Please let me receive whatever comes in life in the wrapper of detachment."

Assessing Real Needs

Many people often have such questions: Is it wrong to have worldly desires? Is it fine to aspire for fame or wealth? They wonder whether material success can ever go hand-in-hand with spiritual growth. They seek to enjoy a perfect life with harmony in relationships, financial freedom and physical vitality. They wish to hone their creative potential and achieve worldly success. But they feel constrained by limitations and fall victim to the uncertainty of life. They lose inner peace in this pursuit of material success.

There are others who seek inner peace and a deeper meaning to life. However, inner peace and lasting fulfillment seems to elude them as they are drawn into the demands of daily living, of keeping up with the living standards of those around them. Hence they feel that spiritual progress cannot accompany material growth.

There is nothing inherently wrong with money or any other object of pursuit. It is the urge of pursuit itself that is wrong. Everything in the world has been created for everyone in abundance. Everything is pursuing us; we need not pursue anything. We only need to be receptive in order to receive these.

We need only be present in the experience of Self-awareness wherever we are—at home, at the workplace, in the marketplace—in whatever we do. When we perform our role sincerely, all those things that are required for our divine purpose naturally come to us. We need not struggle to achieve anything. Our calm receptivity attracts everything that we truly need in our life.

We need to assess our real needs. If we mistake a rope in the dark for a snake, we might search for a stick to beat the 'snake'. Here, the need felt for a stick is not wrong. But we need to question ourselves, "Is the stick really needed?" Since the snake is merely an illusion, the stick is not really needed. If we are making effort to acquire something that deviates from our actual needs, then it cannot give fulfillment. What we really need is a torch that can help see the rope as a rope. Then the need for the stick will vanish.

In the same way, when the ultimate truth about life is comprehended in the light of higher understanding, our needs may naturally undergo a change. We will find that what was a necessity earlier in the absence of wisdom, can be dispensed with.

The utilization of money, skills and qualities undergoes a change when we keep the spiritual purpose in mind. Things, which were earlier utilized for indulging in the illusions of the world, will be utilized for realizing the true purpose of life. Thus, while we continue to engage in the material world and earn wealth and fame, the way we relate to them will change completely.

While we attain wealth and fame, it is also important to acquire vital qualities like patience, resilience, consistency, equanimity, creativity and courage. These qualities are the key to realizing our highest potential. They are the qualities of the real Self. It is vital to develop these qualities through various situations that arise in life.

Wisdom lies in desiring qualities, not material objects. When you desire these higher qualities, everything else follows naturally as a bonus. You will find that money comes to you naturally. You will then utilize money appropriately.

For example, instead of desiring a car, you can pray for the quality of being available wherever you're needed at the right time. What do you gain from the car? The Top Ten (superficial attributes) of the car is ephemeral. It won't satisfy you for long. All pleasure based on superficial aspects withers away with time. By having the car, you actually desire that you can be available at any place that you need to at the right time. Desire this quality of being at the right place at the right time. The vehicle that needs to carry you will automatically come. You need not necessarily own it.

When you desire specific outcomes in relationships, your real need is the qualities of love and harmony. When you pray for love and harmony, it will eventually come. With this clarity, you need not determine specific milestones on the path.

Instead of desiring a good bank balance or a high salary, you can pray for abundance. Abundance is a quality of the Self. When you attune yourself with the vibration of abundance, everything that you need to attain your highest potential will naturally come to you.

When people lack this higher understanding of life, they keep accumulating money and magnifying its value, without putting it to the highest use. This is like a person who keeps polishing his shoes throughout his life, but never sets out on his journey! Money is only a means; it is not an end. We need to keep the end in mind while earning money. We can then attain both–inner peace and worldly success.

10

The Motivation for Karma

We, as the human race, experience so much stress, disappointment, frustration, anger, irritation, depression, and discouragement in our daily lives. How much of all this arises due to one little thing in our heads—expectation? Probably all of it does!

When things don't happen as we would expect them to, or when people don't behave as we expected them to, all such feelings begin to arise. Whenever we perform some action, physically or mentally, we build expectations regarding the result. We wish for instant gratification of our desires, we expect people to respond positively, we wish for praise, approval, thankfulness, respect, recognition, and so on. And when it doesn't come, we sink into negative feelings.

What is the secret to get rid of the pain and anguish that comes after performing an action? The Gita says: 'Perform your deeds without desiring the fruit of your deeds.' Taoism says: 'Act without expectation.' Indeed, this is the secret that helps carry on with our deeds without stumbling upon the block of negative emotions and feelings. Let us first understand how and why this secret exactly works, before moving further…

Each of our actions yields corresponding fruit; this is the law of karma, which nobody can escape. Even if you do nothing and just lie down in your bed all day and all night, you cannot escape the fruit of your action because 'doing nothing' is also an action. If a student decides to relax and not prepare for his exams, failure is inevitable.

If we don't like the fruit of our actions, we will need to change our actions. We perform some karma each and every moment of our lives. Some actions yield instant results while some yield delayed results.

Since many actions yield delayed results, people become frustrated or disappointed and stop performing their actions. It is mainly for this reason that the above secret has been revealed to mankind. As soon as we start doing something either through action or thought, the fruit begins to move into our lives. The thing that our action merits begins to enter our life. Since this happens in the invisible realm, man remains unaware of what is transpiring in nature 'behind the scenes'.

What Happens When We Forgo Expectations?

When we perform any action for the first time, our complete focus is on the action because we don't yet know what kind of result is going to come. We perform the action with a straightforward, intuitive thought, resulting in our best possible performance at that time.

But as soon as we see the result of our action, our focus shifts to the result. We create an impression of the result in our mind. The next time we perform the same action, our focus remains on the past impression of the result rather than on the action itself. We expect to see the same result. Consequently, we do not perform to the best of our ability and the result is invariably different from the previous one, thereby giving rise to negative feelings.

By forgoing the expectation of the result through heightened awareness, we once again think in a straightforward, intuitive manner and perform to the best of our ability. We don't allow past memories to act as speed bumps in our thought process. This is the biggest benefit of forgoing expectations of the fruit of our deeds.

Moreover, when we perform an action as an expression of happiness and do not bother or worry about the result, the action itself brings fulfillment and contentment. If we expect positive results in advance, our action becomes inferior and secondary to the results.

Half-secret

Act without desiring the fruit.

Expecting a particular result causes suffering not only when it remains unfulfilled, but also when it *is* fulfilled. When the fruit is received as expected, it boosts the ego. The ego is reinforced with the belief that it can control the result. The ego tries to fix the outcome of action and attempts to control the result. This causes stress while we perform action. Episodes of non-fulfillment become more painful.

When the expected results do come, it can also cause us to become careless. For example, suppose a student studies just a few days before the examination and clears it successfully. The next time, he becomes careless and studies only at the last moment. The world may call this as 'overconfidence' but it is actually carelessness. What is the use of studying if it is done only for clearing an examination? The careless student may not even clear the examination this time around.

Another reason why it has been advised not to harbor expectations is that there is nothing you can really do about the result once you have performed your deed. Suppose you smile at someone and wish him, "Good morning!" But the person does not respond. He doesn't even smile back at you. Why do you need to expect a smile or a greeting in return? You performed your deed out of joy; that's it. There is nothing you can do to force the person to respond. If you still insist, he may retort by saying, "What is so good this morning?" There are many such people in this world.

So Where's the Motivation in Forgoing Expectations?

Forgoing expectations without completely understanding this principle in the right spirit can lead to negative outcomes such as inertia, dullness and a lack of purpose. It can also lead to various misunderstandings.

A student may say, "Whether I study or not, I will fail the examination. Then why should I study at all!" A spiritual seeker may attend a couple of spiritual discourses and say, "I felt good after listening to the discourses, but two days later I felt nothing great. What's the point! Why attend the discourses at all!" Someone may say, "How can I get the motivation to do something if I don't expect anything good in return?" Someone else may ask, "Why should I work hard at my job if I cannot expect a pay rise in return?"

This is where the full secret comes into the picture.

Perform your deeds and expect not from the channel but from the Source. And expect nothing less than the ultimate fruit—Enlightenment! This is the full secret of how to perform karma. Let us understand this in its depth and entirety.

Take a pause and examine the feeling with which you start new actions. What is the feeling with which a mother starts caring for her child? It is selfless love. The child also gives selfless love in return. But as the child starts growing up and gives lesser attention to his mother, the mother starts resenting his behavior. So should the mother stop expecting love from her child? Should she stop caring for him altogether? Not at all!

Full-secret

> Perform your deeds and expect the ultimate fruit of Enlightenment from the Source.

Stop expecting the fruit from particular channels. You can expect the fruit from the Source, not the channel. The Source, here, means the Self, God, or Consciousness. Expecting fruit from the channel only leads to disappointment. The channel is merely a channel; it is only the medium to deliver you the fruit. Suppose a person who lives in the desert visits you. Impressed with the water flowing through the taps, he says, "I will take a tap with me to the desert. Then we'll never face water scarcity again." What will you tell him?

Does the tap have any capacity of giving? The tap is merely a channel. There are many taps through which water is received, but they all come from the same water source. If you insist that you want water only from a particular tap, then you are inviting sorrow. If one tap closes, ten others can open for you. This is the way nature works.

Be open to receive the grace in abundance from the Source. Rest in faith that the ultimate fruit will come from the Source through some channel at its right time.

In your daily dealings and interactions with people, know that you are actually giving to the Source and receiving from the Source in every transaction, in every communication.

So the mother can continue to perform her deeds but expect the fruit not from the channel (the child) but from the Source (God). She must keep her selflessness alive and continue to give—for what you give to the world, returns to you multiplied! This is a law of nature. Nature has this quality of multiplication; it multiplies whatever you give to it and returns to you. If you offer help to someone in earning wealth, wealth will come back to you multiplied. If you become instrumental for peace in the community, you experience peace in your own life.

How Can Right Karma Lead You to Enlightenment?

To understand how we can avail the ultimate fruit of Enlightenment through karma, we need to understand what karma is and how exactly it needs to be done.

Karma can be inspired by both good and bad intentions. A deed that appears benevolent externally can be driven by a wicked intention. Likewise, a deed that appears wicked outside can be arising from very noble intentions. A mother does not feed her child when he is ailing from gastric disorder. She keeps him hungry. Her act may outwardly appear wicked, but is driven by her loving care!

So it is your internal state of mind that determines the quality of your karma and the ensuing result. Karma performed out of ignorance, which is devoid of higher understanding, and which arises from negative feelings causes bondage. When you repeatedly perform such deeds, it forms tendencies within your mind, which sets you up for repeat performance of the same deed. You become a victim of your own deep-seated tendencies. This is the beginning of karmic bondage.

Ultimately it attracts commensurate results into your life. These results induce similar karma from your side and you again beget similar results, creating a vicious cycle that you get sucked into. This vicious cycle of karma creates bondages that keep you tied down in worldly life and prevent you from moving towards liberation.

To break free from all bondages and rise up to Enlightenment, you need to understand the soul of karma… you need to awaken the soul of karma in your deeds. What is the soul of karma? How can the soul of karma be awakened?

The Soul of Karma is embodied in three aspects—love, understanding and purity of intention. Deeds that are imbued with the Soul of Karma arise from higher awareness. Action that arises from an awakened soul of karma brings completeness and fulfillment in your life. The soul of karma is the door to Enlightenment.

Action arising from ignorance, lower intentions, devoid of love and compassion is soulless karma. It is reactive as it arises from the past conditioning of the mind. It does not give completeness. It entangles you and leads to sorrow or confusion.

The wisdom behind soul of karma lies in the clear recognition of who-you-truly-are. Happiness is your true nature. Focusing on the result is inherently flawed and occurs due to ignorance of your true nature. You postpone your happiness to the future attainment of the fruit.

True joy is never a result of action. Joy is your true nature. You cannot do something to gain joy. Rather the innate joy that is experienced in the awareness of who-you-truly-are naturally touches whatever you do. Joy is a quality of the real Self. When you are absorbed in Self-awareness, you experience unconditional joy. You don't need to do something to gain happiness. Being alive, itself, becomes a cause for celebration. Inspired actions then happen through you, because you are experiencing this joy of aliveness.

If at all you do want to desire a fruit for your actions, then it can be said: *Perform your deeds and expect the ultimate fruit— Enlightenment—from the Source, not the channel.* The aspiration for enlightenment will liberate you from all other desires. It will lead you to stabilize in the experience of the real Self. Hence, if you want to expect anything at all, then desire the supreme fruit— Enlightenment!

Surrender the Action and Also the Result

The best way to stay focused on the deed with an awakened soul of karma is to surrender your actions and the results to God.

Most often, actions are performed with a feeling of doer-ship ("I did it"). We think, "I made this happen" or "Oh! I shouldn't have done this; it's wrong." With such feelings, the individual egotistic 'I' is strengthened and we become bound to the karma and its consequences. Karma performed by assuming the individual 'I' to be the doer causes bondage. If the sense of doer-ship is strong, the action strengthens the tendencies of doer-ship. Such actions are like lines drawn on a rock with hammer and chisel. They cannot be easily erased. Actions performed without a strong sense of doer-ship are like lines drawn in water. They are erased as soon as they are formed.

Actions that arise from the understanding of your true identity, as the untouched consciousness, are the greatest virtue. They arise from a standpoint of non-doer-ship. The understanding here is that actions are just happening spontaneously in the presence of the enlivening consciousness. Such actions are like lines drawn in the sky. They are never really formed! Hence, such actions can never bind you; instead they become instrumental to liberate you from bondage.

Let not your mind grumble, mumble or comment after performing an action. Surrender everything that happens to God, even joy. Surrender even the fruit that comes, whether you like it or not. If you make a habit of surrendering your actions and results to God, then the fruit that you will eventually receive will be the ultimate one—Enlightenment.

All misconceptions, inhibitions and disappointments come to an end when one embraces the full secret of performing karma. Neither stop expecting, nor expect from the channel. Be open to the grace of God. Receive it in full flow because it is available in abundance!

11

The Basis for Result of Karma

Some people are very happy in life while some are totally miserable. Some enjoy great health while some are bedridden for life. Some live in the lap of luxury while some suffer a hand-to-mouth existence. Some have loving relationships in life while some are forlorn, lonely and hateful. The state of our existence today is not random or coincidental. Our suffering and pain are not punishment from an autocratic God. Our present state is simply a result of our past actions. This is the law of karma, made famous by the Eastern religions of Hinduism and Buddhism.

The law of karma states: Every action bears fruit. There is a consequence to every action.

Those who understand this law are able to stop complaining in life and steer their life in the desired direction. The law of karma answers some of the most perplexing questions regarding life and incidents happening therein. Let us try and simplify this highly misunderstood subject – a subject that has baffled the wisest of the wise.

Karma is not fate or destiny. Karma is not something you did in a previous life. Karma is the Sanskrit word for 'action'. Karma simply means any action that has an effect on us or our surroundings.

Karma can be inspired by either positive or negative feelings like love, joy, hatred, malice, anger, fear, ego, attachment, etc. Karma inspired by positive feelings has positive consequences while karma inspired by negative feelings has negative consequences.

All Karma Begets Consequences

The law of karma is meant for learning and evolving. How else will someone learn and grow, unless one learns through feedback from one's own actions? A person undergoes suffering only if he has created the conditions of suffering for himself. Similarly, you experience happiness only if you have created such conditions through your own actions. The law of karma is thus a beautiful arrangement made by nature to help humans understand how life works.

> **Half-secret**
>
> Every action bears fruit. There is a consequence to every action.

Let us understand this with a simple example. Suppose there is a person who is overweight and lazy. He tends to overeat and doesn't exercise his body. And one day he falls severely ill due to the effects of obesity. What is his karma? Eating excessively and not exercising. Due to this habit he keeps eating excessively and keeps avoiding exercise in order to satisfy his bodily desires. Nature then automatically sends him the consequence of his karma – illness.

Why does nature send him this consequence? Because, it wants him to learn that his actions are harmful to his life purpose. Indulging in things that take you away from your true nature can be considered harmful to your life purpose. We are not our bodies; we are the masters of the body, mind and intellect. Anything that we do, that takes us away from our true nature, results in negative results. This is nature's way of teaching us how to move in the right direction. Nature constantly gives us hints in various ways to guide our life force towards its true purpose.

The half-secret that is known to most people is that all our actions (including inaction) bear fruit. If a student studies hard for his exams, his action bears the appropriate result for him. However, if he does not study, the inaction of not preparing for his exams also bears fruit.

It is popularly known that our karma in the form of our actions in daily life are seeds that we plant. Unseen to us, these seeds sprout and move to fruition, bringing reward or retribution to us. Many popular beliefs even extend this cycle of karma as the cause for rebirth. The idea of rebirth is a topic that needs an elaborate discussion, which we shall consider in a further chapter.

Now, with an open mind, let us consider the Law of Karma from a different perspective. Consider that the only consequence of an action is that a 'tendency' is formed. The full secret of the law of karma can be stated as: The feeling associated with action bears fruit. The imprint that is etched in the mind results in consequence. No imprint, no consequence!

The way it works is as follows.

Repeated physical or mental actions program our subconscious mind and create a habit. And hardened habits bring about corresponding results. Thus, the imprint on the subconscious mind automatically attracts the corresponding consequence in life to help you learn through your own choices.

Let us understand this with another example.

Suppose a student fails his exams despite studying hard. He then develops a notion that he fails the exams despite putting his best effort. He feels, "Whether I study or not, I meet with failure. So I'd rather not study at all. It doesn't make a difference anyway." Due to this belief, he does not prepare sincerely for his exams. He then resorts to cheating in the exams. Cheating can bring obvious consequences – he may be caught cheating and reprimanded. But the deeper consequence is often ignored.

As a consequence of this karma, a tendency of taking shortcuts is ingrained in his subconscious mind. If he already has this tendency, the thought of avoiding effort and cheating reinforces it. Subsequently, he will attract situations in his life where he would constantly seek easy shortcuts that may prove to be costly one day or the other. People who limit their knowledge to the external result will call that karma.

How does repeated thinking lead to the formation of tendencies? Let us understand this with an example. You would have seen streams flowing down the hills during the rainy season. These streams follow the same pathways in every monsoon. Why? Because the ridges that are carved by the constant flow of water become more deeply ingrained. When the water was flowing initially, it would have taken effort to clear the obstacles along the way. But later, these pathways provide the easiest ways to flow, as they offer no resistance.

Similarly, repeated behavior becomes deeply ingrained as tendencies in the subconscious mind. Behavior then tends to flow effortlessly along the routes of tendencies, as they have become habits. For example, when one tends to become angry, a habit of being short tempered is developed. As a result, man helplessly expresses anger even when he does not really want to. The pattern of anger becomes more deeply ingrained through its repeated expression. Patterns are formed based on the intention that backs your action.

When actions are repeated in thought, they form subtle impressions on the subconscious mind. These patterns that are etched in the deeper mind are helplessly enacted. One becomes a victim to one's tendencies and manifests them helplessly. This is bondage.

This process has been automated by nature to work on its own. God doesn't decide on a case-to-case basis whom to punish and whom to reward. The human subconscious has been designed this way. Hence, it doesn't matter whether someone believes in God or not. His own tendencies ensure that he will have to undergo the consequences of his karma. If he becomes aware about his own tendencies and clears them, he learns and grows through this process. This is a law and it is applicable to all humans, whether believers or atheists.

So here's the missing link. Even if this student only thinks about cheating in the exams and then puts off the idea due to the fear of being caught or due to guilt that he is thinking something wrong, the consequence of this thought is that his pattern of cheating and deceit will be reinforced by this thought. Even 'thought' is karma. And then one day, he 'actually' cheats. He actually ends up copying from his notes in the examination hall because he has been thinking of doing it in the past.

Thus, one consequence of his karma of thinking is that his tendency is reinforced. Another consequence is that he may end up actually doing what he has been thinking about.

Full-secret

> The feeling and intention behind action bears fruit. The imprint on the mind results in consequence. No imprint, no consequence.

It is important to remember that all actions originate at the mental level. Hence, karma is essentially mental action and the fruit of karma is also at the mental level. Though actions and their results are manifested at the physical level, it is the mental karma in the form of thoughts and feelings that really matter.

Let us consider a few more examples to further elucidate that it is the *feeling* associated with karma, and not the karma itself, that bears the fruit.

A surgeon uses a knife to cut open somebody's body. And so does a highway robber. The surgeon and the robber both perform the same karma. But will they also encounter the same kind of fruit for their karma?

A mother spanks her child for playing with sharp objects. She wants to instill a sense of caution in her child. Another mother spanks her child for trivial reasons just because she wants to vent her frustration. Will both the mothers beget the same fruit for their karma?

One doctor recommends several expensive diagnostic tests to a patient to rule out chances of a bigger disease. Another doctor too recommends the same set of tests but only for extracting money. He knows that there is no need for those tests. Will the same consequences befall the two doctors?

When a judge sentences a criminal to death, will he have to undergo painful implications of his karma? Will the executioner who hangs a convict to death have to undergo suffering because of his karma?

You can clearly make out that it is the feeling behind the karma, rather than the karma itself, that bears the fruit. Positive feelings bear positive fruits and negative feelings bear negative fruits. The purer the feeling behind the karma, the more positive is the fruit.

We often hear people complaining that some people enjoy a great life when their actions seem so negative, and that some others lead a miserable life even though their actions seem so positive. The action that is considered appropriate in a given context can turn out to be inappropriate in another context. The intention behind action determines whether the karma is appropriate. What may seem to be a terrible act to your eyes could possibly be backed by the purest intention. On the contrary, what may seem to be the most benevolent and kind act could be a crafted manifestation of a wicked intention.

So when we have complaints about things or people in our lives, when we keep feeling why we keep suffering in spite of doing some magnanimous acts, then it can help to contemplate upon the true feelings behind those acts.

Some people are sad that their grown-up children have deserted them or have become insensitive to their needs. They complain that in spite of nurturing their children for all these years, they have to face such a calamity today. Such parents should contemplate upon the feelings with which they brought up their children. Did they bring up their children out of true love? Or was the love and affection shrouded by selfish expectations? Did they want to exercise control over their children? Did they treat them as mortgage for old age? They will receive the fruit of happiness or sadness according to the feeling behind their karma, not according to the karma itself.

Some people work a lot for charity and give hefty donations for various causes, yet they feel sad or face misfortunes in life. Why do they receive the negative fruit of sadness when their karma is positive? This is because perhaps the feeling behind their karma is negative. Perhaps they may be unconsciously seeking credit, acknowledgement, appreciation or fame through the act of donating. If their feeling is noble, if they really care for the cause they are supporting, then nothing can ever stop the positive fruit of happiness from coming in their lives.

Then there are some people who have the habit of helping others. They constantly give advice, help with shopping, suggest various things like which doctor to consult, which shop to go, which places to visit during vacations and so on. Yet, they grumble that they don't receive any love, respect or help in return. They feel sad that nobody reciprocates their gestures. Such people should reflect upon the feeling with which they help others. Is it genuine care? Or do they want to exercise control over them? Do they help due to a deep sense of fear and insecurity? Like feeling, like fruit!

After reading about this law of karma, you might get a doubt: If the action itself does not bear fruit, what happens to brainwashed terrorists who kill innocent people in the name of God? What fruit do they get – positive or negative? Even though their action is negative, the thoughts behind it are seemingly positive. They have been brainwashed into believing that they are serving God by killing people. So if their thoughts are pure, will they get positive fruits for their karma?

The answer will be clear if you understand the feeling behind their actions. Even though their thoughts may be 'positive', due to being brainwashed, their feelings are negative – they are fire-bred with hatred for the victims. They consider their victims as the villains of this world. They have deeply negative feelings, which is why it is easy for them to kill.

Therefore, they will definitely receive negative fruits of their actions, even though they believe that they are doing a sacred job. If they didn't have negative feelings, they would never have killed anyone. The fact that they are able to kill indicates the depth of their malevolent feelings.

This example also clearly illustrates the difference between thoughts and feelings. Feelings are at the core of our karma. Thoughts give rise to words and may follow with actions. If feelings, thoughts, words and actions are all aligned in the same direction, the quicker is the result. More the disparity between feelings, thoughts, words and actions, more is the delay in getting the result, because such disparity lessens the intensity of feelings. Ultimately it is feelings that bear fruit; not thoughts, words or action. But it is possible that thoughts, words and action may alter the intensity of feelings.

The Real Result of Karma is a State of Mind

Check your mind after performing any action. Is it happy? Is it sad? Or is it confused? The real fruit can be only one of these three. This is yet another missing link that the full secret reveals.

Consider two students, A and B, who are studying for their exams. 'A' studies very hard and scores 90% marks in the exams. 'B' does not study as hard as 'A' and scores 80% marks. What is the result of their karma?

People usually believe that the one who scored 90% marks has obtained a better result than the one who has scored 80%. However, what if 'A' feels disappointed because he expected to score 95%? And what if 'B' is jubilant because he didn't expect to score more than 70%?

We can see here that it is not the external result that matters. The real result is the internal state of mind that follows. From this perspective, the fruit of karma can be only one of three possible outcomes – happiness, sorrow, or confusion.

When we learn to take results in a stride and surrender the feelings that ensue, we begin to rise beyond expectations. We begin to dwell in the unshakable bliss of our true nature. This is the real purpose of all endeavors.

12

Whatever Happens is for Growth

There was once a man who owned a small convenience store. His earnings barely covered his basic living expenses. He was not happy. Having learned the efficacy of prayer from his Guru, he started praying sincerely for progress and prosperity. But after a few days, he was shocked to find out that a supermarket was coming up exactly in front of his store. Terrified and worried about losing all his regular customers to the new supermarket, he rushed to his Guru and asked him what he should do.

The Guru replied, "Whenever you go for your morning walk, stand before your shop for some time, look at it lovingly and seek forgiveness from it." The man was puzzled. The Guru explained, "You should seek forgiveness from your shop because you were not happy with it. You never thanked your shop for the livelihood it provided. Not only this, but you should also seek forgiveness from the supermarket because you held negative feelings for it, you wished bad for it, and you hated it."

Although the man was a bit perplexed, he obeyed the instructions of his Guru. After a month, he came back to the Guru and told him, "I am closing down my store." The Guru asked, "Why? What happened?" A big smile flashed across the man's face. He informed, "I have been appointed as the manager of the new supermarket!" When the Guru asked him how this miracle happened, he replied, "As you had instructed, I practiced the forgiveness exercise every day during my morning walk. The owner of the supermarket also used to come for his morning walk. As a matter of chance, I met him and became friends with him. He was curious to know what I did with closed eyes in front of my shop and his supermarket. I told him about the forgiveness exercise. He was impressed. Considering my character, politeness and work experience, he offered me this high paying job of the superstore manager."

Half-secret

Everything is a result of karma. Endure it and overcome it.

Why do problems appear in our lives? Why do we run into troublesome people and difficult circumstances from time to time? The popular answer to these questions is that problem situations and hardships that appear in our lives are a result of karmic bondage. We have seen that the tendencies and patterns that reside in our minds invite the various situations in our lives.

However, there is a deeper secret to this. The full-secret is that seemingly problematic people and circumstances can also be a result of your higher prayers.

Challenges are a Doorway to Growth

Some of the events or situations you view negatively are actually the results of your higher thoughts for growth, for realizing your innate potential. For example, if you've strongly held the intention to succeed in your career in a short time, you very well may be confronted with a series of challenges for this to happen. However, when you do not relate these challenges with your intentions to grow, you would probably view these growing pains and the stress related to them negatively.

In reality, they have appeared because of your higher orders. In this case, they are part of your prayers for a rapidly successful career. There are skills, knowledge and experiences you must gain, before you can succeed in your career. Every setback, frustration, challenge, obstacle or struggle, becomes a powerful teacher and an elevating springboard. This understanding will help you entertain only happy thoughts even in the midst of struggle.

> Suppose a little child wants to play cricket but has no one to play with. He insists that his father should play with him. The father is not very interested, but loves his child and doesn't want to dishearten him. So he agrees.
>
> The child prefers to bat and improve his game, so that he can be selected for his school team. What does the father do? Of course,

he will bowl, so that his darling child can practice batting! Not that he likes to bowl, but he would still do it out of love for his child.

Now, the father would love to see him improve his game and be selected for higher league matches. So what does he do? He bowls bouncers and googlies (deceptive spinning balls) at his child. The child feels let down when he is unable to face the ball effectively and protests that his father is unfair. He even complains that his father does not love him, and hence is making batting difficult for him.

The father then explains to his child lovingly that he is raising the difficulty level of the game, only so that his son can become an expert at the game and hit the ball out of the ground with confidence, without being flustered by googlies or bouncers. He teaches his son to read the bowling carefully so that he can hit the bouncers and googlies for sixes and fours.

When the child learns the art of getting on top of the bowling and batting with poise and confidence, he feels grateful for his father's contribution in his success.

In the game of cricket, you need someone to bowl to you so that you can bat. Without bowlers, you can never get to bat and you won't be able to mature into an ace batsman.

This metaphorical game of cricket between father and child resembles the game of life. The father here represents your relationships – your family, friends, neighbors, colleagues, managers, subordinates, your local civic services and also the government! All these people, who play a variety of roles in your daily life, avail you the opportunity to mature and develop vital qualities like patience, uncompromising love, playfulness, consistency, resilience, creativity, steadfastness, to name a few. It is only when you develop these higher qualities that you truly grow and mature and bring about a transformation within and around you.

Actually, the bowler and the batsman are both in the same team. Both are helping each other progress. If you have come to earth to learn and express the quality of courage, nature sends some person or incident into your life that will threaten you or intimidate you. You are supposed to face this person or incident with courage. One day, you will overcome your greatest fear and scale the peak of courage. But since you have forgotten how it all started, you consider the person or situation as your enemy, instead of your own teammate who is bowling the delivery of fear at you.

In the mythological epic Ramayana, Queen Kaikeyi's seemingly evil move actually led Lord Rama to achieve his purpose on earth – that of vanquishing Ravana. In a story from one of the Hindu Upanishads, his father's wrath led Nachiketa to the final Truth of existence. More recently, Tulsidas' wife criticized him to such an extent that he went on to attain liberation from this illusory world and pen the epic Ramcharitmanas for the benefit of humanity.

When someone helps you in a way that's obvious, you feel that he or she wishes you well. However, when someone puts you down, or constrains your progress, or poses problems in your career, you feel they are being unfair by bowling real-life bouncers and googlies at you.

Consider people around you as partners, as contributors, as co-creators in the journey of your life. Those who arouse contempt within you are actually eligible for your compassion. They may be playing a negative role in your life, only because they are co-creators. They are helping you make real progress in life.

Full-secret

> Everything comes as per your orders, your prayers. Whatever happens in life is meant to lead you to progress. Take advantage of it to learn your life lessons and grow.

When do your best qualities get a chance to manifest? When valleys are deep, the hills appear equally high. A blackboard is black so as to highlight the white chalk. When people bowl bouncers at you, you have a chance of scoring runs. The one who wants to become an expert at this game of life doesn't fear the bouncers of setbacks or difficult situations. He knows that these are opportunities to score well in the game of life.

When you receive every situation and person with this understanding, you will feel grateful for everyone and everything that seems like a problem to you. You will thank those people and situations.

What if someone told you, "[So-and-so] task is impossible for you…?" You can either quit, or let a surge of passion and willpower drive you to accomplish that task. You may have seen people react positively in such situations. They say, "No matter what, this is something I *have* to do now." The thing to remember here is that the person who ridicules you or tries to pull you down is in fact your own teammate. He is bowling to you to help you practice. He loves you and cares for you. Those batsmen, who remember who the bowler is, play the game cheerfully. They even thank the bowler for providing useful practice. But those batsmen who have forgotten who the bowler is always grumble and sulk in life.

Consider the game of chess. It cannot be played alone. You need a partner to play chess. He makes one move and you make the next move. This is what makes the game interesting. Will you lose your temper or feel sad if your partner is making tough moves? No. You will simply be eager to raise your own game. By playing tough, your partner is only helping you to raise your capabilities and feel good about it.

The game of life is no different. Even if someone is defeating you again and again, you are not supposed to get sad, worried or angry. If you do get sad, worried or angry, it means you have not understood the game at all. The reality is that your opponent is actually your partner, your own teammate, who is helping you awaken your dormant qualities. If you are constantly facing troublesome people and incidents in life, understand that it is all an arrangement for you to rise up and win the game.

Understand the secret that people or circumstances are not your enemy. They are not a source of trouble. They have arrived in your life to give you a gift. You have to take your gift. Until the time you keep resisting troublesome people and circumstances, you will continue to be tormented by them. So stop resisting and start receiving. Receive your gift. Learn your lesson. Raise your capabilities. This is the full-secret. Once you receive your gift, the troublesome person will change and the troublesome situation will turn favorable. Their role was to just give you your gift. Nothing else! Your relationship with problematic people will turn loving and sweet once this role is over.

If you avoid taking your gift, people and circumstances follow you wherever you go. They don't breathe easy until they hand over the gift to you. They keep coming back at you. Handing over the gift is their purpose in life. If you run away from them, they have to keep chasing you. The only sane thing to do is to meet them and receive your gift gracefully. Only then will they relax and go about their own business.

If you reflect upon your own past, you might stumble upon incidents that exemplify this secret. Perhaps you had strained relations with certain people, but those very relations improved after you learned some valuable lesson. Maybe some people are no longer part of your life, but they left after providing you some valuable wisdom. You may have realized that wherever there was acceptance, relationships were sweet. And wherever there was resistance, relationships were bitter.

The one who understands that the bowler and batsman are in the same team, no longer has negative feelings for anyone. So contemplate upon your life and identify your teammates. Be grateful for the role they are playing in your life. Thank them, at least in your mind. The divine plan that the Source has for you is to realize your full potential. People who appear in your life are part of this plan. Whenever we resist situations or people, we fail to see the Source (the father) functioning through them. We fail to see his love. Henceforth, be assured that it is but our own divine father who is bowling at you.

The Divine Plan of Infinite Possibilities

People ask questions about destiny: Is it in our hands to shape our destiny? If God is deciding our destiny, then are we limited to achieve only as much as we are destined for? They assume destiny to be a chalked-out life where everything is pre-determined and limited.

The real question to be asked is: What exactly is our concept of destiny? In whose hands is destiny? Who do we consider ourselves to be? And who is God?

Behind everything, it is God's hand alone. Everything is happening by His will – the Divine will. And by Divine will, the potential of our destiny encompasses everything in this universe and beyond!

Many people live with the limiting belief that "I get only as much as I am destined for." This notion is based on the belief of scarcity. But there is a deeper belief that gives rise to this notion – the belief that we are individual body-minds leading individual lives. When we are attached to this false idea of self, we see limitations and scarcity and entertain a feeling of lack. Such a belief leads to competition and an unconscious notion that we have to take away from others in order to get something. The belief of scarcity makes people feel that "If I have to win, others should lose."

The universe is teeming with unlimited possibilities. The world in which we live is wonderfully obliging. Everyone can win! The supreme creative potential of the Self makes it possible to fulfill the wishes of everyone simultaneously. We need to allow 'faith in abundance' rather than 'fear of scarcity' to steer our lives. There is abundance of everything for everyone.

You are already destined for everything that you could possibly need in this lifetime. There is abundance of love, peace, bliss, health and wealth in your life and also everyone's life. There is a natural flow of money, time, happiness, and harmony in your life and everyone's life. However, the belief of scarcity blocks the natural flow of abundance.

You naturally progress toward your higher potential in life, so long as you do not place obstacles in the free-flow from the Source. This is the divine order of the universe.

The question to be asked is: "Will it be in my capacity to receive whatever I am destined for? How can I eliminate my negative feelings and limiting beliefs and harmonize with the free-flow of the Universe to fully receive whatever is in my destiny?"

Even if we were able to draw a minutest part of the infinite potential that we are destined for, what a life we would enjoy... A life brimming with love, joy, peace, wealth, health and creativity! We will be wonderstruck at what's in store if we transcend our limiting beliefs based on the false idea of who-we-are.

When you realize who you truly are, when you realize your true nature as the Source of everything, your body will be too less to experience the sheer magnitude of bliss. You will say one body is not enough... you need more bodies to fully experience that bliss. You will begin to spread the joy. Thus, you will see that your destiny actually spans much beyond your individual needs to benefit many people.

Whatever We Give, Returns Manifold

Every action that happens through us is like a seed that is planted in the field of consciousness. Consciousness nurtures and transforms these seeds into fruit. The Universe functions as a multiplier that multiplies the seeds that we sow. Whatever we invest with the Universe is augmented multifold. The resulting harvest depends on the quality of the seeds that are planted. The Multiplier works and multiplies all the seeds irrespective of whether they are from a beggar or the emperor.

It is very important to be happy when we plant the seeds through our actions. We have seen that our feelings are the real seeds that we plant while acting. Our external actions are not as important as the internal feeling that we are in. The seeds of our feelings germinate and bring respective results. Positive feelings provide immense positive charge to the seeds.

Even if we can do nothing about negative seeds that have been planted in the past, it is the seeds of feeling that we plant today that govern our future. We create our future with the feelings that we choose in every situation that we encounter each day.

Hence, we need to be vigilant that we don't plant weeds of sorrow; we should be intent on planting seeds of happiness in the present.

It helps to develop the habit of frequently asking, "Am I planting seeds or weeds? Am I singing in harmony or grumbling in discord?" This will help in raising awareness about your feelings. If you find that you are not attuned to the divine flow, you can attune yourself through such questioning.

Give your best to the Best to get the best. Sow the best seeds. A farmer is well versed with this principle. He knows the importance of sowing the best seeds. After planting the best seeds, he tends to his fields, provides them water, nourishment and care, and leaves the rest to the Universe. Once the harvest is ready, he collects the crop and again segregates the best seeds from the harvest. The best seeds are planted again to improve the harvest. In this way, the quality of the seeds and the harvest keeps growing.

This is the secret of infinite growth. Learn and familiarize yourself with this secret. Sow the best of your seeds. When results manifest, you receive a multifold of what you had given. Again from the new gifts you've received, re-plant the best ones in the Universe to get even higher quality of results. This is Faith in Action.

OUR BELIEFS SHAPE OUR DESTINY

Due to ignorance of the Divine law of abundance, many people live with false notions. Some say, "You will gain only if you work hard," others say, "Wear these good luck charm or this lucky gemstone and your fortune will change for the better."

We only need to learn the art of planting healthy seeds through the right thoughts so as to bring forth the grandeur that we're destined for. It is our thoughts that contribute the most in determining our lives. The feeling that we live in shapes our lives.

When people find their life changing by using good luck charms or gemstones, *Fengshui* or *Vaastushastra*, it is largely the change in their beliefs that works to bring about the change in their fortune. The external elements only serve as pretexts to alter their beliefs.

Those who are bound by a victim-mindset tend to believe whatever their sun-signs or horoscopes foretell. When we go beyond a mechanical way of living and consciously choose how we want to live, astrological readings can no longer bind us. There is no question of being lucky or unlucky, happy or unhappy. Who-we-truly-are is the source of luck, the wellspring of happiness.

Thus, the full-secret is that everything that happens is designed to help you make progress in life. If you have prayed for self-progress, nature throws difficulties at you so that you can develop the qualities necessary for overcoming those difficulties.

Let every situation remind you that it has come for your higher progress. Everything that is happening in life is for your growth and to bring completeness. Remembering this will help you tide through rough situations with ease and perseverance.

You need to harbor positive feelings for the people and situations that pose problems. It is easy to get angry, hateful and bitter at them. By doing so, you plant weeds for your future. By remembering that they have arrived in your life to help you, you will receive every circumstance gracefully.

13

The Magic of Forgiveness

Forgiveness is one of the most powerful responses that we could ever give in life. Forgiveness is not merely about apologizing or accepting apologies; it has a deeper aspect to it. Forgiveness is a matter of the heart; not words. Forgiveness involves sensitivity, awareness, compassion and love. Those who love themselves do not hesitate to either give forgiveness or seek forgiveness.

Forgiveness can completely wipe away hatred, resentment and ego. It increases the purity and piousness of the mind. Forgiveness is a conscious, deliberate decision to release feelings or resentment or vengeance towards someone who has harmed you.

Why Forgive?

When we assume ourselves to be the limited body-mind, it gives birth to the illusory notion of 'others'. This naturally gives rise to delusion, resulting in emotions like anger, fear, greed, hatred, envy, ill-will and resentment.

When we entertain such negative emotions in ignorance of our true nature, we actually resist the flow of life through our bodies. Negative, hurtful memories, bitterness, and ill-will choke the free flow of life within us. When one holds onto grudges in life and feels bitterness and resentment, it clogs the free flow of life. Eventually this affects our physical wellbeing, causing chronic ailments in the longer term.

By feeling resentment towards any person or situation, we actually plant further seeds of hatred. We unknowingly pray for even more resentment that rebounds back on us, multiplied many times over. We do this in ignorance due to lack of awareness.

Half-secret

> Forgiveness is about forgiving everyone completely, even though we may feel bitterness for him or her, even though we may have every logical reason to resent him or her.

The first person you may have forgotten to forgive is yourself! Most people tend to be difficult on themselves and lack forgiveness for themselves. They are unwilling to forgive themselves. There is no need to dwell in the guilt of past misgivings. They should be cleared and forgotten.

If we experience bitterness and have cursed how life has treated us, then it is essential to forgive ourselves. There are people who blame God for the tragedies in their lives. Their child may have died young; they may be rid with sickness; they may be going through financial struggle. Consciously or unconsciously they complain and blame an imagined God for all this. There is deep-seated resentment; yet we cannot experience miracles when we are holding resentment towards God. We have to rid ourselves of bitterness. We must question ourselves, "Am I blaming God for my situation?" We need to forgive ourselves to absolve ourselves of these pent-up grudges that we have for life itself.

We have to get rid of resentment, also towards those closest to us. Close family members like the husband, the wife, children, parents – all must be forgiven when resentments have built up in family situations. Many people say, "I didn't think that mattered. I thought that it's normal to have all this in the family." We have to sincerely practice forgiveness, especially with every family member.

And there has to be forgiveness for anybody, who has ever done anything hurtful for you. You may feel that your bitterness is justified. You may perhaps believe that the person has done something seemingly terrible. You may have every legitimate and logical reason to hold a grudge and to hate the person. But if you wish to see miracles in your life, it is absolutely imperative that you forgive.

Forgiveness cleanses you. Forgiveness is the key. Forgive them to the point where you actually feel yourself cleansed of resentment and bitterness and are actually praying for them. If you do not, the lack of forgiveness will make it impossible for you to experience true freedom.

Forgiveness brings the forgiver peace of mind and frees them from corrosive anger. Forgiveness does not mean condoning or excusing a serious offence that someone may have committed against you. You need not reconcile with the person who seriously harmed you if you don't want to. But the definition of forgiveness definitely includes letting go of deeply held negative feelings. In this way, it empowers you to recognize the pain you suffered without letting that pain overpower you, enabling you to heal and move on with your life.

Forgiveness – The Eraser of Karmic Bondages

So far, we have seen the importance of forgiving ourselves and everyone else for grudges and negative feelings that we have held within us. But this definition of forgiveness is only the half-secret. The complete reality of forgiveness encompasses a much deeper and wider dimension.

Forgiveness is an all-curing panacea for all the negativity and problems that fill your life and that of the whole world. How? It is because forgiveness erases karmic bondages, the basic cause of all misery in the world. Forgiveness clears out our karmic bondages and fills us with divine love, joy and peace.

Moreover, those who practice forgiveness enjoy better mental and physical health. Diseases cannot find favorable conditions to grow in such people. Such people easily free themselves from problems and live a life filled with happiness, prosperity, health, success and cheerfulness. Whatever our aim in life may be, forgiveness practice is the master key to its door.

Seeking Forgiveness – A Responsible Practice

> A manager leaves for his office in the morning. On the way, a dog happens to bite him. Furious, he reaches his office and shouts at his subordinate over a petty issue. The subordinate becomes upset over the unnecessary rebuke and vents his anger at the office boy, asking him why he hasn't brought him his cup of tea yet. The office boy gets irritated and shouts at the tea vendor asking him to hurry up. The tea vendor thrusts the tray into his hands, turns to his son playing around his legs and hits him for interfering in his work. The son gets angry and flings a stone at the same dog that bit the manager. Now the dog sets off in search of a new person to bite.

In this story, it is clear that each one, involved in the sequence of events, has contributed to the negative feelings arising in others. The negativity in the world too is a result of each inhabitant's contribution. Each one of us is responsible in some way for everything that occurs in our awareness, in some way or the other. Let us understand how this happens.

If we seek forgiveness from God for our negative contribution, and also seek forgiveness on behalf of our fellow brothers and sisters, the entire world's negativity can be finished. This is what forgiveness is all about.

The Contamination of Pure Consciousness

Consider a sheet of paper on which words are written. The paper exists behind every word and also between every word. The words cannot exist without the paper.

If we draw parallels to human life, we see that there are numerous individual life forms, but the background of all these – the Universal Self or Consciousness – is one. Pure Consciousness is the source of all manifestation. It pervades and enlivens our physical and mental existence. Individual human life is merely a part of the expression of the 'whole' on the screen of universal consciousness.

Suppose you write on a sheet of white paper. There is a carbon paper placed beneath this sheet, resulting in impressions being formed on another white sheet of paper below it.

Here, the carbon paper represents the collective mind of humanity. Whatever thoughts or emotions we entertain, cause impressions to be transferred through the universal mind (the carbon paper) onto universal consciousness (the white paper below it).

When we assume ourselves to be an individual body-mind, it gives birth to the illusory notion of 'others'. This naturally results in emotions like anger, fear, hatred, depression, resentment, complaints, blaming and frustration. When we entertain such negative emotions in ignorance of our true nature, we resist the flow of life. Negative, hurtful memories, fixations about people, bitterness, and blame choke the free flow of life within us. Eventually this affects our physical, mental and social wellbeing.

With every act in our past where we have either felt hurt or caused others to feel hurt, we draw lines of bondage on the screen of pure consciousness. These lines of bondage block the free flow of life through us.

When you resist the free flow of life, you experience testing circumstances, limitations and sorrow. Thoughts, feelings, words and actions that have arisen from the ignorant belief of separateness bind you and choke the expression of life. This is the manifest form of karmic bondage.

Actually, these limitations and suffering come as wake-up calls to re-connect and re-align with the natural flow of the Self. They come as reminders to recognize and honor the essential Oneness of everything.

Full-secret

> True Forgiveness is about seeking forgiveness for everyone including yourself. It is about forgiving yourself. You are responsible for everything that occurs in your field of awareness.

You need to get rid of these karmic bond by performing actions that assert the truth of who-you-truly-are. This will open the doors to liberation from action. You will then effectively continue to perform the highest actions without incurring any karmic bondage.

True forgiveness is meant for erasing these karmic lines that tie us down in the rigors of worldly life and relations, preventing us from moving towards liberation. Every time you develop impure and negative feelings for someone, a karmic line gets drawn on the whiteboard of pure consciousness, linking the two of you in a karmic bondage. Most people today have thousands of lines all around them, thereby obscuring the purity of consciousness that permeates the world.

Greater the hurt you cause to people and greater the negative feelings you keep within your mind, thicker are the lines of karmic bondage that tie you down. Even if you think the other person was at fault and not you, the moment you develop negative feelings for them in your mind, a line of karmic bondage gets drawn on the whiteboard. Since most people in the world are unaware of the laws of karma, they keep piling lines upon lines and as a result the universal consciousness of the world has become polluted.

The best way to remain free from karmic bondages is to not create them. For this you will have to raise your awareness to such a level that as soon as you get the slightest hint of negativity arising in your mind towards somebody, you will instantly erase it. But until you get to this level of alertness and awareness, you can start by erasing the lines everyday, preferably at bedtime. Also, you will need to get rid of the thousands of lines already present on your whiteboard. Even if a single line remains on it, your liberation is at stake.

Now the question is: how to erase our lines of karma? How to free ourselves from the umpteen problems and difficulties of life and move towards total liberation?

The answer: with the practice of seeking forgiveness. The complete practice of forgiveness consists of seeking forgiveness from people, giving them your forgiveness, seeking forgiveness from yourself, giving yourself forgiveness and seeking forgiveness from God for yourself and on behalf of others. The emphasis here is on seeking forgiveness for yourself and also on behalf of others.

Forgiveness is essentially an internal practice that functions at the mental realm. Hence, it suffices if we sincerely seek forgiveness mentally within ourselves, with the other person or situation. We need not necessarily seek forgiveness by speaking to the other person physically, though we may do so if we feel comfortable.

Hereafter whenever you sense a problem or negative situation at home, or your workplace, or in the country or in the world, perform forgiveness prayer as follows:

Dear God,
Please forgive me for whatever little contribution I have made
to the given problem situation through my feelings and thoughts.
Please forgive me for not recognizing your presence
while harboring anger, resentment, hatred, and complaints.
Please forgive us all for our contribution to the situation.
Thank you for freeing me from bondage.

If you sincerely do so, not a single line of karmic bondage will remain on your whiteboard of pure consciousness and you will start experiencing divine love, joy and peace.

The earlier you perform the forgiveness exercise the lesser effort you will need to remove karmic bondages. For example if drops of tea fall on your shirt, the earlier you wash the shirt, the easier it is to remove the stains. Cleanse yourself every day with the practice of forgiveness. Recall incidents of the day in which you kept negative feelings for someone or hurt someone. Your mind may tell you that it was their fault, not yours. But no matter whose fault it was, the bondage has already been formed because of the feelings in your mind.

The best way to seek forgiveness from people is to go up to them and directly ask for forgiveness. But if it is not possible due to awkwardness or some other reason, you can definitely do it mentally. Bring those people before your eyes and seek forgiveness mentally. Also forgive them for the hurt they may have caused you. Pray to God, seek forgiveness and tell yourself that henceforth there is no need to entertain negative feelings because you are in favor of love, not hate. No matter what happens, you will remain in favor of love.

Remove Your Contribution to Problems in the World

During childhood you may have played the game of making a house of cards. If you remove even one card from the stack, the whole house starts collapsing. The negativity of the world is like one big house of cards, and all of us in the world have contributed a card each. The whole house of negativity can be razed to the ground just by removing our card from it. And the practice of seeking forgiveness is the way to remove our card. Forgiveness has the power to solve all the problems of the world. At the outset you may perhaps not believe it, but once you begin the practice you will subtly comprehend its impact.

First of all, we need to change our perspective of looking at problems. If we are making a negative contribution to it, we need to become aware. It is natural to think, "If there are potholes on the roads, what did I do…? If corruption is increasing, what is my fault…?" Now we know that everything is a combined effect of everybody's thoughts. Maybe our individual contribution could be very little; perhaps just 0.0001%, but we have to remove our card anyway, by seeking forgiveness. We have to remove our individual negative contribution and increase our positive contribution.

Not to be Blamed, But Being Responsible

It is important to bear in mind while seeking forgiveness that you are not doing so because you are to be blamed, but you are being responsible. You seek forgiveness because you are a responsible presence who is willing to heal the negativity that plagues the collective psyche of humanity. You take responsibility to cleanse the whiteboard of consciousness by erasing lines of bondage that appear in your awareness.

It is important to understand that you are not overlooking others' actions when you seek forgiveness. Instead, you are healing the situation and freeing yourself from the karmic bond that grips you and consciousness as a whole. You are seeking forgiveness from the Source, from consciousness, because it has been tainted.

Hereafter whenever you see a problem at home, outside, in the country or in the world, perform forgiveness prayer as follows:

> *Dear God,*
> *Please forgive me for any negative contribution*
> *that I have made towards the problem through my thoughts and feelings.*
> *Please help me to accept myself...*
> *Please help me to forgive myself...*
> *Please help me to love myself.*
> *Thank you for freeing me.*
> *Thank you... thank you... thank you!*

In this way, remove whatever little negative contribution you have made towards the world's negativity. Instead, contribute positive, creative and noble thoughts to the world. If each one of us does this, the negativity can be eliminated, paving way to positive creations.

Shift to a Universal All-Inclusive Perspective

Those who have faith in prayer know that their prayers are being heard and answered. What will happen if we change words like 'I, mine, for me' in our prayers to 'we all, ours, for all of us'? Will not our prayers be answered? Of course, they will. If prayers done with 'I' are answered, prayers done with 'we all' will also be definitely answered. Then why not include all of us in our prayers? Why not say, "Please forgive all of us" instead of "Please forgive me?"

Lift prayer from a personal level to an impersonal, global level so that everyone can benefit. This is the ultimate form of forgiveness practice. If the whole world benefits, we shall also definitely benefit because we are also a part of the world. If the rays of the sun fall on everybody, your share of the sunrays does not reduce. Likewise, if the grace of God falls on everybody, your share of grace does not reduce.

There are some people in the world who practice forgiveness for everybody and for all the problems in this world. They contribute positive thoughts to the world. They pray not for themselves but for the betterment of the whole world. Whatever good and positive that you see in the world today is because of such people! Progress in society happens due to such an all-inclusive presence.

As a Tejgyan initiative, hundreds of thousands of people pray regularly at 9.09 a.m. and 9:09 p.m. every day for world peace. If you too join them, you can send your contribution of healing vibrations and loving thoughts to those who need it.

Imagine divine white light falling upon Earth and the golden light of higher consciousness emanating from it. All the negativity of the world is being removed. Everyone is receptive to love, joy, peace and forgiveness. Everyone is opening out and blossoming.

If it is not possible for you to pray for everybody right now, at least pray for solutions to your own problems. Seek forgiveness for all your negative thoughts and remove your card so as to contribute positivity to the world.

14

Rebirth and Liberation

Reincarnation is the idea that death is not the end. It is popularly believed, predominantly in eastern cultures, that the living entity drops the body upon physical death and is reborn in a new body after a temporary period of rest. Reincarnation is an integral belief of many spiritual traditions, but not all.

We will find that most western traditions believe in a linear flow of life, where there is no idea of reincarnation. Once earth life is done, the linear flow philosophy says that the departed being abides in the afterlife thereafter.

Eastern traditions follow the philosophy of a cyclical pattern of life. The cyclical pattern is based on the idea of the opportunity of learning and growing across multiple births.

But why is reincarnation necessary? The main reason is seen as the opportunity it provides to make slow steady progress towards fulfilling the highest goals of life.

The Rationale Behind Reincarnation

The reincarnation philosophy suggests that we take the essence of experiences and lessons learned from each incarnation and move onto new births. In this process, the individual soul grows through a comprehensive learning from many varied experiences in multiple lifetimes.

> **Half-secret**
>
> The soul is reborn in physical embodiment to clear its past karma and learn vital lessons to progress towards Moksha. Upon Moksha (the Ultimate liberation), the cycle of rebirth and death of the physical body comes to an end.

For example, we may learn about the temporary nature of material things. In another incarnation, we may learn patience. We may learn to trust others in yet another lifetime, so on and so forth.

Another rationale behind reincarnation is that with the onset of physical old age, our bodies become old and tired. We become incapable of taking fresh challenges and learning new lessons. When the aged body declines and becomes a limitation, it does not serve the purpose of fulfilling our learning aspirations. Rebirth then affords us a fresh embodiment to learn these lessons.

Yet another purpose of reincarnation is the law of karma. What goes around comes around. "As you sow, so shall you reap."

Reincarnation provides a platform for the law of karma to function. It facilitates learning through results of past karma that can span across lifetimes.

At the culmination of the series of rebirths, we reach a point in evolution where we realize our oneness with the Source of all creation. This has been given various names like *Nirvana*, *Moksha*, Emancipation, *Mukti*, etc. It is believed that at this point, the soul escapes the cycle of birth and death and is never reborn thereafter.

This is the understanding that has been passed on across many generations of eastern tradition. Most people hear about it; some believe it, while some don't. However, most people decide to believe about reincarnation without any sound investigation or rationale. And this is where the full-secret provides a transcendental view of the matter.

The Myth of Rebirth

Does reincarnation actually happen? Are we really reconciling our karma from previous lifetimes? Such questions arise in people's minds, but few attempt to go deeper into the subject and gain clarity.

The question to be asked is: Who is actually born? Whose karma is it? Who is experiencing all this?

The belief in reincarnation arises when one is stuck with the limited perspective of the human body without understanding the grand game being played behind the scenes. The concept of rebirth is a fiction arising from the limited standpoint of individuality, of personhood.

When one realizes the standpoint of the Self, rebirth will lose its meaning.

Let us understand this with the help of an analogy.

Suppose you place your hand into a pot to feel the various things kept inside. As you put your hand in the pot, each finger touches a different thing. One of your fingers touches mud, another touches a flower petal. A needle pricks the third finger while the fourth finger feels the softness of cotton wool. Each finger gets a different kind of experience.

But, who is actually deriving the experience? Are these experiences limited to the fingers alone? No. It is for the one who has placed his hand in the pot to derive all these experiences. The one who is outside the pot receives all the experiences.

The fingers in this analogy represent human bodies. Man feels that he is experiencing the various facets of life. But in reality, the universal Self, who is outside the manifest world, is the experiencer of everything. Whatever good or bad is happening, it is the Self alone who is receiving all those experiences. The Self wishes to gather a diverse range of experiences through mankind.

Who is actually performing karma through the human body? The Self, alone, is performing karma through all bodies. And the Self, alone, is receiving the fruit of all karma.

A child is born when the Self begins to gather experience through the child's body. The Self exists before the birth of the body as well as after its death. The Self is beyond birth and death.

You can compare the physical body to building material used for construction. Buildings are built, inhabited and later demolished. The building material, however, can be re-used further. If one looks at life from the perspective of the building, then there is construction (or birth) and demolition (or death). However, from the standpoint of the one who builds, uses, and destroys the building, there is no birth or death.

Coming back to the analogy, the experiences that are gathered through the fingers are stored in memory. Suppose one of the fingers perishes. Consider that the hand grows another finger inside the pot. The one outside the pot re-uses the experiences of the perished finger from memory, and implants it in the new finger.

In other words, the experiences gathered by the Self through a particular body are available in the form of memories. The Self re-uses memories gathered from one human lifetime by planting them in further bodies.

When the individual (the finger) is unable to make sense of certain memories that are being played out during this lifetime, he believes that he has been reborn. He believes in the concept of reincarnation. Actually, there is nothing like reincarnation. All incarnations are of the Self alone. The Self is unborn. Yet it experiences birth through all bodies.

What is the ultimate motive of the Self behind gathering experiences through mankind and re-using them? The purpose of re-use of memories is to bring about healing and progressive evolution. The Self evolves through the re-use of experiences in subsequent bodies.

You can see that every new generation of mankind is ahead of the previous generation in terms of their level of understanding. This happens because the Self uses whatever experiences are gathered from a given generation to better the succeeding generations.

Full-secret

> The Self re-uses experiential memories gathered from one lifetime in subsequent human bodies for healing and progressive evolution. *Moksh* (the ultimate liberation) is the liberation from the birth and death of the individual ego. It is the dissolution of personhood.

This is why we find that children of each generation are cleverer than their predecessors. Inventions in each generation have paved the way for further inventions in the generations that follow. You would have heard of child prodigies who demonstrate wondrous skills early in their childhood. There are three-year olds who can play the piano skillfully, children who are able to solve complex mathematical problems effortlessly. This demonstrates how the Self reuses memories of experiences drawn from previous bodies.

Through this process of progressive evolution, the Self explores its boundless potential. The Self reaches the pinnacle of its evolution— the state of Self-realization and expression of its divine qualities. One who does not know this game of the Self assumes it to be the rebirth of a previous human body. Man believes that he is evolving whereas, in reality, it is God who is evolving through each human form.

During the multitude of lifetime experiences that the Self has gathered through human lives, there are also injured memories – memories of pain and trauma, fear and suffering endured through the bodies. The Self also plants such injured memories within subsequent human embodiments for the purpose of healing.

These injured memories can surface during the lifetime on earth in testing situations. However, when we assume that we are separate individuals (fingers of the hand in the analogy), we are troubled by the pricking experiences that come our way. We take these memories personally without realizing they have been planted only for healing and release.

Man keeps grumbling that his life is filled with suffering. He keeps complaining: "Why me! Why am I going through such bitter experiences? I have helped my people, but no one helps me."

He should be asked, "Who are you?" The separate individual is only a false idea. All the experiences are the Self's alone. If he helps his neighbor, it is like one finger helping its neighboring finger. Upon Self-realization, clarity dawns that the hand is helping itself through the interplay of all its fingers. All help is Self-help!

When we are denied help, it is an opportunity to unconditionally express love. The opportunity is to learn, mature and evolve to a state where we realize ourselves as the source of unconditional love and compassion.

When one contemplates on this paradigm shift and builds conviction in it, it can be truly liberating. All the suffering and grudges that we hold can vanish if this truth is understood.

Moksha – Liberation from the Individual Ego

It is easy to understand the real meaning of Moksha or Nirvana from this perspective.

Let us understand it with an analogy. Consider the ocean and its endless waves. The waves rise and fall back into the ocean. Though they may appear to be individually separate, waves do not have an individual existence of their own… unless it is imagined to be so. Each wave is essentially the movement of the ocean itself.

Drawing parallels to human existence, each human body-mind is a wave of expression of the Self. Bodies come and go, just as the waves rise and fall. But the Self, like the ocean, lives eternally and expresses incessantly through the human mechanism.

The wave is merely a form of expression of the ocean. But when the ocean identifies itself with a particular wave, it gives rise to an illusion of separateness, a notion of individuality. The wave assumes itself to be a separate entity.

In the same way, an illusion of separateness is born in the human body. This illusion can be called the individual ego. The ego is merely an appearance. Actually it is the Self that is expressing through the body, assuming a separate personality.

The ego rises several times every day during the lifetime in the body. It considers itself separate from other human bodies. This is like one wave standing apart from other waves. The ego is the cause of all defilements like anger, boredom, sorrow, jealousy and fear.

When the Self in the human body-mind receives wisdom, the ego begins to dissolve. The feeling of separateness dissolves and is replaced by the feeling of devotion. The underlying oneness of all beings is experienced. Moksha or Nirvana is the permanent death of the ego. This is the missing link.

The prevalent widespread belief is that Moksha is the end of the cycle of rebirth of the individual. The truth is that the individual does not exist at the first place! It is the ego that likes to fantasize an eternal future for itself. It wouldn't like to die. So it imagines that it will be re-born as a new body.

When the Buddha attained enlightenment, this is exactly what he proclaimed, "O builder of the house, I have now clearly spotted you. Never again will the house be built." What is the house in this case? It is not the human body. It is the individual personality that is built by the ego. When the Buddha says that the house will never be built again, it means that the ego will never rise again.

15

Spirituality Beyond Occult Practices

We live in highly challenging times. We work longer hours and often compromise on life balance, feeling more stressed and hurried than ever before. We're being bombarded with choices, both significant and trivial, that demand a great deal of effort and energy.

These days, we're inundated with information that demands urgent attention and action. These unprecedented demands cause us to expect too much from ourselves. This quickening of life in the technological age has also distanced us from the ways of nature. We have fallen into discord with nature's rhythm, compromising on harmony and balance, which are so vital for our wellbeing.

When stress accumulates beyond the threshold that our bodies can take, we suffer burnout. When we do not pay heed to the build-up of stress in our body-mind mechanism, it develops into chronic physical ailments like hypertension, diabetes, heart disease, obesity, etc.

In order to counter this, knowledge about alternative ways of relaxing and healing our body-mind systems are becoming popular by the day. The last two decades have seen an unprecedented increase in demand for alternative healing therapies, yoga and mindfulness practices, besides other energy modalities. A plethora of therapies and practices are becoming popular.

> **Half-secret**
>
> Awakening *Kundalini*, Healing with energy modalities, *Tantra* and yoga are spiritual practices.

Some of these therapies and practices do bring benefits in healing and restoration of the healthy natural state of the mind and body. It is believed that dealing with the human body-mind mechanism at the psychic plane or energetic plane is more effective than physical plane.

Practices of mindfulness have become so popular that courses in mindfulness have been mushrooming all around the world. Mindfulness relaxes the mind and body and sharpens mental faculties. Yogic practices and therapies have also become the order of the day in ensuring physical fitness and mental wellbeing.

However, there are certain occult practices like breath-work, *Tantra*, *Kundalini awakening*, *Shakti kriya*, and other similar techniques, which have been prescribed for healing and catharsis. So far, so good, but the unfortunate news is that these practices are being commoditized and offered under the banner of 'spirituality'. And this is where the full-secret needs to be unraveled.

THE MYTH OF SPIRITUALITY BASED ON OCCULT PRACTICES

The half secret that many people are aware of is the practice of *so-called* spiritual cleansing through breath-work, awakening the *Kundalini*, energy healing etc. These practices may have their own benefits. They may possibly help in healing traumas; they can perhaps help as alternative techniques in healing body ailments. However, they have nothing to do with spirituality at all.

Spirituality has been corrupted due to misguidance. The real purpose of true spirituality can never be acquired in the world. One of the sad drawbacks of these occult practices is the belief that spiritual growth, which involves dedicating oneself to work within and realize one's true nature, can simply be replaced by a bunch of rituals and traded like a commodity.

People are made to undergo rituals in the name of spiritual cleansing with lofty promises of enlightenment. Mystical experiences and psychic perception are sold in the name of spirituality. It is one thing to be curious about paranormal phenomena or supernatural occurrences. But when these are categorized as 'spiritual practices', then the real purpose of spirituality is missed.

Full-secret

> True spirituality is beyond energy, mind, and matter. It is beyond the known. It is the subjective experience of pure consciousness. It is about realizing who-is-experiencing-all-this.

Such occult practices deal with the human psyche, energies, or the body. True spirituality is beyond the mind, beyond the realm of energies, and beyond the physical realm. Hence, no amount of dabbling with these practices can ever lead one to the purpose of true spirituality.

As an example, let's consider the case of the practice of *Kundalini* awakening. Kundalini, in simple terms, is the latent energy that is believed to be present in the *chakras* (vortices of the human energy body). It is believed that this latent energy can be awakened through specific practices and rituals of transfer of energy. It is claimed that this leads to the manifestation of mystical powers.

> There was a hermitage of a Guru in the middle of a forest. There was no proper roadway to reach the hermitage. To add to the difficulties of reaching there, was a swamp on the way. The Guru used to teach how to walk using stilts to all those disciples who wished to come to the hermitage. (Stilts are two stout poles with footrests in the middle, used for walking high above the ground).
>
> Initially, the disciples used to fall off quite often. But they were made to continue practicing. With regular practice, they

gradually learnt to walk using stilts. Now the uneven terrain or the swamp was no longer an obstacle for them. They could now easily reach the hermitage.

However, at this juncture, many disciples became content with learning stilt-walking, and forgot their original purpose, which was to reach the hermitage. They were happy to just walk on stilts. Only those disciples who reached the hermitage and showed readiness to listen to the truth were imparted further knowledge.

Similarly, gaining mystical powers through occult practices has nothing to do with the real purpose of spirituality. The desire for *siddhis* (mystical powers) is a huge distraction in the way of Self-realization – the true purpose of spirituality. It is possible that you may develop certain mental or perceptive powers in the journey. But if you get stuck with them, you lose out on the ultimate goal.

Acquiring psychic powers does nothing but inflate the ego. The more you serve your ego, the farther you drift from your Self. The purpose of life is not at all fulfilled by acquiring psychic powers like face-reading, mind-reading, pineal gland activation, *Kundalini* activation, etc. In fact, such powers pose a huge block in the way towards Self-realization.

Enlightenment – Beyond the Manifest World

True spirituality is beyond energy, mind and matter. It is the most obvious experience of who-you-truly-are, and yet it is unknowable to the mind. To understand the real purpose of spirituality, it is essential to look at the origin of all creation.

The original state of the Self is a state of rest, when the world is not created. It is an unexpressed state where the Self alone exists, where only the subject exists. This is the state when the experiencer is present, but cannot experience the experiencer itself. This is the Self-in-Rest. This can also be known as Shiva – the primordial state of unexpressed potential.

When there is only one without another, one cannot know oneself. It is only when there is *another* that one can feel one's own presence. So as to experience the Self's own presence, the Self-in-Rest brings about the state of Self-in-Action… the expression of the Self. The subject creates the object so as to experience its own presence.

This expression manifests as energy-in-action. It takes the shape of thoughts and of the world as we perceive it. When the Self manifests as energy, it is the state of Self-in-Action. Self experiences itself through this expression. This expression can be called Shakti – the expression of Shiva, the dance of Shiva. The state of Self-in-Rest is the pure screen of consciousness and the Self-in-Action is the colorful film projected on this screen. The Self-in-Rest is the unchanging, boundless and the untouched observer. It is the essence of everything.

The Self-in-Rest is like a dancer who begins to dance so fast that he cannot be seen clearly. All that is visible is the hazy expression of dance – the Self-in-Action.

One will not be able to appreciate the presence of the dancer, as one is lost in the expression of the dance. As one has not seen the dancer before the dance commenced, one remains stuck in the various aspects of the dance.

When the Self forgets its true nature, it gets identified with the mind and body. It assumes "I am the mind, I am these thoughts, I am this energy, I am this body." Due to this false identification, the real purpose of experiencing the original state of Self is forgotten. This is exactly what happens with people who get entangled in practices related to energy, mind and matter. They tend to focus on the expression of energies and work to manipulate energies and acquire powers.

When awareness is trained to return onto Self, it becomes possible to clearly spot the dancer in and through every movement of the cosmic dance. In every experience, the focus will be on the dancer –the Self-in-Rest–without whom, the dance would not happen!

While looking at a mirror, if you do not see yourself, then the purpose of the mirror is not served. In the same way, while witnessing the world, the focus should shift to the Self. The interest should be solely transfixed on knowing the Knower. The world serves as a mirror to bring awareness of the presence of the Knower.

Focus on Knowing the Knower of All Experiences

Many people believe that one can behold the brightness of a thousand suns after awakening of *Kundalini*. Such beliefs complicate spirituality. Awakening the *Kundalini* is only related to the body. Be clear that it has nothing to do with Self-realization. Self-experience is the simplest and most obvious experience, which is always going on. Its utter simplicity becomes a problem for the mind that likes to fantasize it.

The mind aspires to know and measure everything in its own terms. The experience of Self is the source of life. It cannot be known or measured by the mind's scale.

Even if the body experiences mystical sensations, or sees some divine light, it is very important to understand this: In which light was that divine light seen? You need light to see anything. However, there is also the invisible light in which you can see light itself! This invisible light is that of awareness, the inner knowingness. It is beyond the realm of sights, sounds and sensations.

When that light is witnessed, awareness is aware of itself. The light of consciousness, which shines upon everything, becomes self-illumined. The Self experiences its own presence. You do not have to get stuck at these experiences of light or sound because the true experience of the Self lies in experiencing consciousness, which enables seeing and hearing.

Everything that is being known is temporary; they come and go. It is the ultimate knower alone that is permanent. The objective world has a beginning and end. Your body and mind too have a beginning and end. However, that which enlivens all this, that which is the knowing presence, has no beginning or end.

Shift your attention from the body-mind to the real experiencer – the Self. Turn back your attention from the objects of perception to that which enables perception, from thoughts to that which enables thinking. You will then rise above the changing and limited to that which is changeless, eternal and boundless.

Awakening is nothing but the awakening of consciousness. The way the energy moves up or down the spine or all around is immaterial to realizing consciousness. The ego creates new distinctions to feel special. Awakening to who-we-truly-are has nothing to do with such distinctions as it leads us beyond the dimensions of physicality and energies.

Experiences that seem to be very gratifying and pleasurable to the mind are major hindrances. The experience of pure awareness is your original nature, and it is always accessible to you. You need not look for any other experience. It is not dependent on the chakras of your energy-body.

A true Guru knows such risks that can entrap the seeker of Truth. He prods the seeker to move further beyond the entanglements so that the seeker transcends the realm of body and mind and gets established in the Self.

16

Self-Experience – Beyond Duality

Since ancient times, Self-realized souls have institutionalized places of worship. In all religious faiths, places of worship have been designed and consecrated so that people can take time out of their daily chores and occupation to devote themselves to the veneration of God.

A place of worship is intended to create an atmosphere that kindles devotion in the hearts of people. The temple or mosque or church has become synonymous with the meeting-place with God. Devotees attune themselves to the divine vibration at the place of worship. This has led to the idea that God can be found at the place of worship.

The underlying belief is that God is the Supreme Being, who exists *outside* the phenomenal world. The deity at the place of worship is representative of this Supreme Being. People practice devotion of idols and pictures that venerate the Supreme Being in various forms.

Half-secret

> God exists outside the world... Idols or pictures of deities are essential for devotional worship. Self-realization is the experience of oneness with everything.
>
> or
>
> God exists within us. Recognition of the formless reality is the purpose of true wisdom. Self-realization is the experience of nothingness.

Congruent to this belief is the idea that God-realization comes with the experience of oneness with all of His creation. These seekers work to establish themselves in the feeling of oneness with all living beings. The concept here is all-inclusiveness. It is about expanding the sense of 'I' to merge with totality out of love for God and His creation.

Much contrary to this, there are people who follow the philosophy that God exists within human being. These seekers may not necessarily believe in external representations or places of worship. They seek God in the silence within. The concept here is of *Neti-Neti* (not this, not that) where everything is excluded. They seek the experience of pure nothingness through the practice of meditation.

These contrasting approaches to seeking God have caused a divide among these ideologies. Adherents of both these ideologies fervently justify their reasons for following their respective approaches.

These two approaches are like the two sides of the coin. The full-secret unravels the third side of the coin, which transcends both.

Beyond Inside and Outside

In the earlier discussions, we have seen that the human body-mind is a medium through which the Self experiences itself and expresses its divine qualities. Self-experience is constantly going on within every living being. It is what lends life to the human expression.

When you consider that the experience of the Self is constantly going on within each of us, it is likely that you might imagine that the Self exists *within* the human body. Though this may be considered true logically, the truth is that the Self is not just within the body. Rather, the body exists within the Self, though this may sound illogical!

The nature of God is pure consciousness, which is source of all creation. Pure consciousness is unbounded awareness. It pervades all of existence. It is everywhere. The body-mind lives in it. At the same time, consciousness lives through the human body.

Think of a fish living in water. Water is an all-pervading presence for the fish. It is the essential medium that keeps the fish alive. Water exists not only within the fish, but also all around it. Water is so close to its eyes that the fish doesn't realize that it's in water. What if the fish swam off in search of water, asking, "Where is water?"

This is precisely what the questioning mind would ask when it is told about the all-pervading nature of consciousness: "Where is this consciousness? Is it within me, or elsewhere?"

The experience of consciousness is your very essence. If you carefully observe, you will find that the spatial concepts of *within* and *outside* are relative to your body and belong in the realm of thoughts. From the standpoint of the Self, there is neither a *within* nor an *outside*. The Self is undifferentiated beingness.

Take the example of a clay pot. When the walls of the pot are made, then there is empty space inside the pot and also outside the pot. Are these two empty spaces different? No, they are one and the same.

Similarly, if you consider the walls of the pot as your body-mind, then what part of the pot do you use? Do you use the walls of the pot, or the empty space inside the pot? The walls of the pot only help in realizing and using the empty space. In the same way, your true essence is the spacious awareness, not the body.

You say that you were born on a certain date. When you realize that the empty space is the 'real I', then will you say, "I was born"? The empty space, which you essentially are, has always been present. When you realize this, you will say, "I have not been born at all. I am unborn" If 'I' is never born, then can 'I' die? Then you are beyond birth and death. Pots will be made and broken down, but the space in which they exist lives on eternally.

The Self needs the body-mind to experience its potential, just as space needs the clay walls of the pot to realize its potential. Let the clay walls become the temple for worshipping the space within and around it.

In other words, let the body-mind serve as a temple to worship God. When devotion for the Truth deepens, the devotee makes his body-mind a pure and sacred temple for the worship of the formless Lord. In divine love and surrender, the devotee is prepared to rid his mind and body of all vices and tendencies.

Beyond Nothing and Everything

The experience of the Self is that of *nothing* with the potential of *everything*. It is not the no-thing that the mind imagines as the absence of something. It is the Nothing that encompasses everything.

> **Full-secret**
>
> God exists beyond the concepts of 'within' and 'outside'. The human body-mind can serve as a place of worship. Truth transcends the concepts of form and formlessness. The Self is Nothing with the potential of Everything.

An apple seed sprouts and grow into a big tree, which produces countless seeds, which in turn grows into a vast forest! If you break open the original seed and look within, what do you find? Nothing! And yet, it had the potential of an entire forest within it.

In the same way, the Nothing is the un-manifest source of all possibilities. It is the creator of the manifest universe.

The mind and intellect try to grasp Nothing in limited terms, which is not possible. The moment we say that the Self is the experience of Nothing, the mind tries to create a picture of Nothing. The moment it pictures it, it is *something*, not Nothing.

In the same way, when it is said that the Self is the potential of everything, the mind tries to posit "everything". It is beyond the bounds of the human intellect. So that the mind does not conjure up any image or idea of this, we can call it "Nothing-Everything".

When the mind surrenders all its beliefs and notions and insistence to know, what remains is the experience of Nothing-Everything.

Beyond the Duality of Forms and Formless

There are people who do not believe in attaining the Truth through the medium of forms. They do not agree with those who believe in a God that has form. Both are unable to see the one Truth.

Both these factions are actually watching the same movie. The first half of the movie depicts a God that has form and the latter half depicts a formless God. Form is an essential means to realize the formless. The Formless cannot be known without a Form. And a Form cannot exist without the formless. With the direct experience of the Self, the duality of form and formlessness is resolved into the one reality that encompasses both.

God has been given many names and portrayed in many forms. But all names and forms point to one thing, the formless truth. Idols and pictures are an essential pretext created by Self-realized souls so that beginners can appreciate God and proceed on the journey.

Some people like one form of God, others like another. Therefore, it's no surprise that we have more than 330 million deities in India.

Most of these were created by the Self-realized souls with the intention, "Let various reminders be created. If you cannot relate to one deity, worship the one you like, but start worshipping." Perhaps, the human population in those times for 330 million! So every human being could be considered as God manifest!

Different deities were created with the intention that one should like at least one face of God, the one that inspires one to take the first step.

At the initial stages in the journey of seeking God, idols and pictures help in kindling devotion. The form helps in worship, because perceiving the formless might be difficult at the outset.

The mind that seeks God needs to understand that God cannot be seen in terms of a defined physical reality. When the mind is infused with this understanding and develops faith in the existential all-pervading nature of God, it surrenders its insistence to experience God or consciousness based on its own imaginations.

Once you experience God as the living consciousness within this body, it will be easy to recognize Him outside this body too. You will recognize God's presence as the consciousness within all forms, both living and non-living. Myths and stories create a misconception that God incarnated only in certain bodies. But everyone and everything in the universe is His form alone.

As one progresses on the journey, one rises beyond the appearances and form. The formless truth begins to reveal itself.

17

Align with the Divine Will

Those who grow both spiritually and materially, who are successful, for whom life seems to flow easily, intuitively know and abide by certain universal laws, even if they cannot put them into words.

Just as there are physical laws that govern the world phenomena, there are also laws that work in the mental realm that determine what we create and experience in life. These laws have existed since the beginning of time and precede the appearance of human life. They are unchanging, universal and apply to everyone, without exception. These laws operate relentlessly and impartially, regardless of whether you feel wealthy or deprived, irrespective of whether life seems to be a success or failure.

One who ignores these laws is at risk of driving the vehicle of life without knowing its consequences. When we operate in life, abiding by the Laws of Thought, these laws begin to work for us.

In order to transform our lives, we must be aware of our thoughts and use them wisely. It is in our best interest to contemplate these laws of thought and act deliberately according to their guiding principles, rather than letting them work randomly by unconsciously misdirecting their forces.

The primary law is the key to creating the life that we want. According to this law, we should focus our attention only on what we want. Think only in accordance with the outcome that you want to experience in any situation.

Half-secret

> You are the master of your life. Pray to the universe with faith and passion for what you desire. The universe fulfills whatever you focus on with faith and passion.

The thoughts arising from within you are nothing but orders that you pass to the Universe. Everything happening in our lives is in accordance with these orders; be it the things that we receive, or the situations that we experience.

Everything you focus on—good or bad—will eventually manifest in your life. Whatever thoughts or feelings you give your attention to, is like placing an order for more of the same. It's important, then, to direct your energy to positive feelings and on what you want, instead of negative feelings of fear or worry about what you don't want.

The Universe fulfills everyone's wish, however it does not understand the word 'no'. When you focus on the thought, "I want to be healthy," you will become healthy. But if you were to focus on the thought, "I don't want to fall sick", then the Universe manifests sickness in your life.

The Universe works on every word that arises in our thoughts. Every thought that we entertain, translates into a result. If this is true, then we need to be vigilant about our thoughts, feelings, words and actions to ensure they are pure, positive and optimistic. There shouldn't be even a bit of negativity in what we project to the Universe.

Backing your positive words with positive thoughts is a vital link in implementing this law. It is indeed an art to use the right words so as to pass the right orders (prayers). This can be mastered by consciously practicing this law.

For example, instead of saying, "I do not want to be bound", say "I want freedom". Our subconscious mind does not understand the words 'no' or 'not' as it cannot picture these words. At some point in time during our lives, we all would have experienced that undesirable incidents have happened with us just because of our incorrect use of words.

Instead of saying, "There should be no corruption in society" or "I don't want to be with bad people" or "I don't want to fall sick", use positive statements such as, "There should be honesty in society", "I always want to be with good people with the highest level of consciousness", or "I want to lead a healthy life, full of vitality", etc.

It is imperative to pass the right orders with a strong faith and conviction through the use of positive words. Even if you carry the slightest doubt while passing orders, it can hamper the achievement of the desired results, making all your efforts futile.

This law has become increasingly popular in the last couple of decades as the Law of Attraction. There are countless coaches all over the world who run courses on manifestation techniques.

However, there is a missing link here. Discussions on the law of attraction and manifestation fall short of explaining the deeper nuances of life. They do not give satisfactory answers to how we can experience a life of permanent and boundless bliss. Many have attempted and claimed that the positive-thinking paradigm does not help to fully account for the unexplainable predicaments that arise in life.

Stop Chasing Shadows

Being able to manifest what you desire does not necessarily guarantee lasting happiness. This is the missing link in the practice of manifestation techniques based on the law of attraction. Without understanding this missing link, it is common for people to get into frenzy with manifesting their desires by using the power of thoughts, believing that it would deliver lasting happiness.

Since thoughts are used as the key to manifesting what we desire in life, we rarely get the thought of unlocking this key! Those who have been able to unlock the secret of thoughts have attained the ultimate treasure of life. They have reveled in the experience of boundless bliss, unconditional love, and unbroken peace. They have expressed the highest creation of life.

The only way to experience true and lasting love, joy and peace is to abide in the Source of everything. Accessing and abiding in the experience of Self is the key to the ultimate treasure of life – a treasure that is already present within you.

There is nothing wrong with the pursuit of material aims in life, so long as one does not remain stuck in them. Behind every human pursuit is the yearning for the experience of unconditional love, boundless joy and unbroken peace. The truth is that love, joy and peace have always been present within each one of us as the essence of our true nature. It's just that we seldom notice and experience them within.

When people lose the experience of true love, joy and peace within them, their pursuit turns outward in the material world. Love, happiness and peace, which are qualities of who we truly are within, are invested in things of the outside world. Satisfaction in external pursuits is instant, but temporary.

Trying to find true fulfillment in external pursuits doesn't work. In the insatiable quest to amass more and better comforts, people lose their value for true love, joy and peace. It leaves them hungry for more and so they remain dissatisfied all the time.

It is like trying to catch the head of your shadow. It always eludes you. Catch hold of your head itself, and the shadow is automatically caught! When you seek true love, happiness and peace within, you discover their source within you – the ever-shining presence of the immaculate Self.

What you are seeking outside is like a shadow. It can never give lasting fulfillment. Your outer world only reflects your inner world. When you stabilize in the experience of Self-realization, you are one with the Source of life. You abide in the experience of the Self. Your life automatically reflects it through the expression of love, joy and peace in the external world.

The Self is Enlivening this Story Called "My Life"

Imagine a painter who paints the picture of a paintbrush. This paintbrush comes alive and serves to create more paintings for the painter. However, if the paintbrush assumes its own individual existence and a separate personal purpose, it would go about painting without consulting the painter. Though it was created to explore and manifest the painter's creative inspiration, the paintbrush will do everything else without seeking to fulfill the painter's wish – the very purpose for which it was created.

In the same way, the human body-mind mechanism is the Self's creation, which serves as an instrument or medium to manifest the Self's further creations. However, human beings perceive and operate individualistically instead of allowing the Self to experience and express through them. Though a lot of creations may be happening in the visible realm, they are devoid of true and lasting fulfillment, since the Self's real purpose remains unfulfilled.

Consider a sheet of paper on which letters are written. Each written letter contributes to the overall story that the author wishes to express. However, if any single letter were to decide to express itself differently, then will the story flow as the author intended? If a single letter were to look around the sheet and compare itself with the other letters, it may find some letters that are bigger, some that are *italics*, some that are **bold** and hence standout. This letter may then feel dejected by comparing thus and wish that it should be like or even better than the others. However, unless the letter attains the perspective of the author or surrenders to his will, the very purpose of why it was penned on the paper is lost.

If we draw a parallel to human life, we see that individual human life is an expression on the stage of life, contributing to the overall plan of the scriptwriter. If any person gets into the game of comparison and the need for superiority and enacts such tendencies, it becomes an abnormality, a deviation to the grand plan of the creator.

To understand this further, consider another analogy. All the parts of a machine, whether small or large, are merely its parts. They do not function for themselves; rather, the machine functions through them.

Due to ignorance, the parts of the machine could perhaps feel that they are functioning for themselves and that they have an existence independent of the machine. But they would be mistaken, because you can clearly see the machine functioning as a whole. The parts are merely instrumental for the purpose of the machine. The story of the parts is partial reality. The purpose of the machine is the complete reality.

In the same way, the Self functions through all of us, through our body-mind mechanism. Being ignorant of this, we as human beings assume that we are leading independent, individual lives, separate from the purpose of the 'whole'.

To put things in the right perspective, when we think, breathe, and are self-aware, the Self lives through us. We are no different from the Self.

We believe that we are leading life. The truth is that consciousness enlivens this story called "my life". This is a paradigm shift in our understanding of our reality.

> **Full-secret**
>
> The Self is living out a story called "my life". The human body-mind is a medium for experience and expression of the Self. Let the body-mind be the instrument for divine will.

When we consider ourselves separate from this enlivening principle, we limit ourselves to birth and death. When we become one with life, we allow life to blossom and express through us. Let us allow life to happen, rather than pre-determining criteria about how life should be. This brings us the experience of lasting love, joy and peace, which also spreads its fragrance to those around us.

You may ask, "Does this mean that we should just go with the flow? Then we become like dry leaves swirling here and there in the wind?"

Contrary to this, when you realize your oneness with the Self, you attain a state of true freedom. You reach a standpoint where you see the drama of life unfolding and direct life creatively.

When we truly comprehend the grandeur of the Self through direct experience, we gain insight into the infinite potential of the Self that is waiting to express through us.

Leading the life of a limited individual without knowing our true nature is like a lion mistaking itself to be a sheep. In doing so, we limit the expression of our true potential to miniscule proportions. It is like using the strength of a powerful elephant to hold a matchstick!

In today's increasingly fast-paced world, man experiences a lot of stress, misery, anxiety, demands and struggles. While pursuing happiness and peace, many are not happy or at peace with themselves. By accessing and abiding in the Self, you can let go of all struggle and live in the faith that your highest possibility is unfolding as per your divine plan. The most powerful creative potential begins to express itself through you.

When you begin to abide in the experience of the Self, its wonders will be revealed. You will begin to gain insights that could never be conceived within the limitations of the human intellect.

Great creations are possible when we are rooted in the experience of the Self. This is because the Self expresses fully through bodies that are receptive, and through which innovations can be manifested.

18

Essence of Spiritual Practice

Spiritual growth revolves around the arduous practice of *Sadhana*. Seekers of Truth work to purify the mind, so that it can be attuned to the divine vibrations of the Self. The ten major vices that render the mind impure are: Anger, Attachment, Boredom, Fear, Greed, Hatred, Ill will, Jealousy, Lust, and Sorrow.

These vices manifest helplessly as a programmed reaction, leading to the creation of karmic bondages. Try as much as we may, there come situations when we give in to these negative caustic emotions, which consume us. Every time we manifest these vices, we suffer remorse and frustration.

Half-secret

> Spiritual work involves getting rid of all vices such as fear, anger, hatred, lust, etc.

By going through the ill effects of these vices, man learns to consciously choose love, joy, compassion, devotion and peace over these vices in testing situations.

When we choose to respond creatively rather than reactively, it causes a dent to these vices. Such persistent practice of *Sadhana* weakens the vices. But this is a slow and arduous process that purifies the mind and annihilates the ego.

Consider a tree that has a big trunk and some branches. The vices like anger, hatred, or greed are the branches of the tree. The ego is the trunk. The vices arise from the ego, just as the branches arise from the tree. Anger, boredom, greed, hatred, lust and sorrow are offshoots of the main ailment – the ego.

ADDRESS THE ROOT CAUSE OF THE VICES

The prevalent practices of *Sadhana* attempt to work on the individual branches; tackle the vices individually. The drawback with this approach is that when one branch is severed, the other branch shows up. When we try to control a particular vice, say anger, another vice overpowers us. This is like a snake with multiple heads. When one head is severed, it raises another ugly head.

> In the Indian epic, the Ramayana, Lord Rama tried to kill the demon king, Ravana, by shooting arrows at the ten heads. But every time a head was severed, a new head would replace it. However, when Lord Rama shot the arrow at his navel (the root), the demon-king met his end.

This story is symbolic. Each of the ten heads represents the ten vices. Shooting at the navel implies uprooting the entire tree, instead of trying to cut down individual branches. We need to tackle the root of the tree – the real ego. When the ego comes to an end, all the vices automatically dissolve. They cannot exist without the ego.

The ego is like a shadow, which does not actually have an independent existence. It is the product of a false identity that the Self has assumed for itself.

Suppose a statue made of salt insists that it wants to measure the depth of the ocean. What will happen? When the salt-statue dives into the water, it will begin to dissolve. It merges into the water and experiences oneness. In the same way, when the ego is made to enquire into the nature of reality and its own nature, it begins to dissolve.

The ego cannot annihilate itself. Can you lift yourself up into the air by holding yourself? No. In the same way, the ego cannot cause its own end. It has to be first transmuted into a positive form. The ego can be transformed into a devotee of the Self by imparting the right understanding. With the right wisdom, the ego dissolves in the experience of oneness with divinity.

True Ego and False Ego

When we look deeper, we will see that there are two egos – the true ego, and the false ego. The true ego can be considered as the root of the tree. The false ego is the trunk that grows from the root. The true ego gives birth to the false ego.

The false ego can be easily recognized as it manifests itself as the vices. Anger, hatred, jealousy are expressions of the false ego. However, the true ego, being very subtle, is not easily grasped. It is hidden and not obvious. To bring down the tree, it is important to tackle the true ego.

The true ego is the subtle feeling that "I am separate from the rest of creation; I am separate from all other beings." The nature of the true ego is separateness. This is not easily discernable. It is the root cause of the illusion.

When the true ego, which is based on the idea of being a separate individual, feels that it is special, it gives birth to the false ego and all the vices. Obstacles like lust, anger, greed, desire, fear, hatred, comparison, and worry may continue to rise in daily life situations. However, the real obstacle is the true ego.

Most people continue to focus on the obvious false ego. The true ego goes unnoticed. Even if they are able to quell the false ego for some time, it will rise up again, because the true ego is hideously still alive.

Your true nature is pure consciousness; you are beyond the mind and body. However, when you are not aware of your true nature, you believe that you are a separate individual, limited to this body. The wave assumes that it is separate from the ocean. This is the original sin. Everything else that is popularly regarded as sin is just the cascaded effect of this original sin.

Most spiritual practices deal with methods of eliminating secondary or derived sin – defilements like anger, hatred, fear, anxiety, etc.

These are the symptoms of the original sin. Merely working to resolve these symptoms cannot lead to liberation, as the original sin, the root cause, has not been dealt with. When we receive the understanding of our true nature and abide in it, we put an end to the root cause of all suffering.

The Contrast Mind – The Tool of the Ego

Our mind is originally like pure water, which clearly reflects the presence of the Self. However, it becomes impure when impregnated with thoughts of the individual 'I'. It is these thoughts that are the filth of ego. The intake of impure water is harmful to health. Just as pure water is vital for the health of the body, similarly it is essential to have a pure mind that reflects the presence of the Self.

All of us have an aspect of mind that can be called the Contrast mind. During infancy, every child abides in the experience of the Self. However, as the child grows, typically beyond 2 to 2½ years, the parental programming and social conditioning lead to the formation of the contrast mind.

The contrast mind is that facet of the mind that discriminates, compares and judges everything. It is the constant chatter that ceaselessly comments about everything that is experienced. Just like the contrast control on a TV remote, which is denoted by a circle with black and white halves, the contrast mind too dwells in duality.

The contrast mind divides everything into silos, and labels objects, beings, or circumstances as good or bad, happy or sad, black or white, dark or light, positive or negative, low or high, benefit or loss, and so on. It dwells in fixations of duality. It draws assumptions about everything. Whenever we notice ourselves thinking: "This shouldn't have happened... That should have happened... Why does it always have to be me? Life is so difficult... When will these people change", it is this contrasting aspect of the mind that is at work.

The other facet of the mind is the intuitive mind, which functions spontaneously based on natural intuition and inspiration. Unlike the contrast mind, the intuitive mind is focused on the present task and performs it to the best of its ability. It is free from comparison, judgment, labeling and fixation. Thoughts of the intuitive mind are harmless and constructive.

When you are scurrying down the stairs, it is the intuitive mind that is functioning. It happens spontaneously and rhythmically. However, while going down the stairs, if you get a thought, "I am climbing down the stairs so well... Uh oh... I only hope I don't trip and fall", this is the contrast mind in action.

Invariably, when the contrast mind comes in, you may have found that you tend to either miss or jump a step, disturbing the rhythm in which you were climbing down the stairs.

The contrast mind causes us to be stuck in the vicious cycle of polarities such as joy and sorrow, love and hatred. This facet of the mind is caught up in imagined notions, presumptions and beliefs. As a result, it triggers fear, worry, anger and depression. It is this facet of the mind that dwells in past memories or the imaginations and anxieties of the future. Due to this, the present moment is lost to us.

These characteristics of the contrast mind do not allow us to accept the present moment as it is. Non-acceptance of the present moment is the root cause of all sorrow. It is due to the judging and vacillating nature of the contrast mind that people suffer from insomnia and are forced to consume sleeping pills.

The contrast mind veils the Self. It is like the eclipse that hides the ever-present sun of consciousness. It is a facet of the mind that causes sorrow. Hence it needs to be transcended to restore true happiness, peace and higher consciousness. Thoughts of the intuitive mind will continue to function through the body.

Hurdles Posed by the Contrast Mind

The contrast mind poses hurdles in Self-experience. There are some major roadblocks that are posed by the contrast mind.

1. Expectations

The contrast mind tends to make a tangible goal out of everything that is pursued. However, the experience of the Self is not a tangible goal. It is the enlivening presence in which all pursuits of life are undertaken. Hence, positing a goal and defining expectations cannot lead to the experience of the Self.

Since every external pursuit in life is quantified or qualified in material or tangible terms, the contrast mind tries to set expectations for the purpose of experiencing the Self as well. It will desire to experience such objectives as peace of mind, tranquillity, deeper intuition, or greater creativity. If it doesn't immediately see such results, it feels disappointed. It then gives up by assuming that the pursuit is impossible or futile.

The key is to see through all such expectations as the play of the contrast mind. Being the Self is the way and the end in itself. You are already at the destination during the journey. You just need to be present, and allow any such feelings or thoughts of expectations to pass by. Let feelings of disappointment or frustration arise and pass by, for they too are food for the contrast mind.

2. Boredom

The contrast mind has no role to play when you are in the presence of the Self. As a result, it may cause feelings of boredom. When you are seated in meditation, a few minutes might feel like you've been sitting for an hour. If you are unable to accept this, the meditation may seem difficult to practice and you might consider giving up.

Continuing to practice being in the stillness of Self-experience despite uncomfortable feelings brings its reward. We shouldn't resist feelings of boredom, but rather accept them as a part of the practice. We should continue to watch such feelings as a detached witness. As we persist, such feelings of boredom will pass away, revealing the experience of stillness.

3. Fixations

Many a times, we may feel we have had a particularly pleasant or unusual spiritual experience. The contrast mind then holds onto this past impression and expects to experience it again. In doing so, it tries to predetermine the experience of the Self. It constantly compares the present experience with past impressions and causes dissatisfaction. It tries to fix the end result.

We should not be fixated about any one thing. Allow whatever is happening to happen, and let whatever is not happening not happen. The purpose is not to know any particular experience, but rather to experience the knower of these experiences.

4. Checking

When we practice meditations to experience the Self, the contrast mind can masquerade as a checker and attempt to judge the experience. The contrast mind assesses, "Is this experience the same as the actual experience of the Self? After sitting for so long, why am I not becoming thoughtless?"

The mind tries to divert our focus from the experience of the Self by checking, comparing, and judging. If we get entangled in this, we lose our attention on the Self and instead become entrapped by the checking contrast mind.

Whenever the contrast mind intervenes and tries to check on the experience, know that it is a trap. The presence of the contrast mind veils the presence of the Self. The mind, which judges and questions the experience, cannot exist without the living presence of the Self. The very fact that the contrast mind is raising doubts and judgments is only indicating the presence of the Self. Whenever a checker thought arises, simply smile and observe it. Know that the mind is playing a trick. Understand that we don't have to question our awareness; we only need to be present in awareness.

5. Taking credit for the experience of the Self

With the experience of the Self, the contrast mind tries to take credit for having experienced it. An expert pianist is rendering a symphony on the piano. When the performance reaches its peak, the pianist is lost in the performance. He does not exist at that time. All that exists is the performance. However, after the performance, the contrast mind enters and says, "I performed so well!"

By taking credit as being the performer, the contrast mind self-appoints itself to the job of experiencing the Self. The Self can experience itself only when the contrast mind surrenders.

Whenever the contrast mind tries to take credit, we should realize that it is yet another trick. Tell the mind, "You cannot own the experience. It is only in your absence that the experience of the Self is revealed. Surrender yourself so that the ceaseless experience of the Self can be revealed. To the extent that you are in stillness, the experience will shine forth. The more you chatter, the greater the delay in the experience of the Self."

TACKLING THE CONTRAST MIND

The tendencies and traits of the contrast mind are played out in the dark, when you are not aware that it is happening. When you bring your awareness into the play of the contrast mind, it leads to clarity and recognition.

Full-secret

> Spiritual practice is meant for getting rid of the hurdles of the judging and comparing mind. When you dis-identify from the false 'I' that you have assumed for yourself and gain recognition of who-you-truly-are, the defilements begin to dissolve.

Detached witnessing enables you to distance yourself from the mind and its works. When you are attached with the mind, you lend it energy. When you witness it detachedly, the patterns of the contrast mind begin to lose their power. However, the intuitive mind continues to function at its best.

The key here is to not resist the mischief of the contrast mind. Accept and allow the whims of the mind to surface. Watch them as they rise and fall. This, in itself, lays the contrast mind to rest. The mind begins to turn inward and get attuned to awareness. It begins to love and accept the truth of what is, as it is. Such a mind begins to abide in the present, without vacillating in the past or future. This makes it conducive for Self-awareness. The pure mind serves as a mirror for the Self to experience itself and express its divine qualities.

19

Transcending Knowledge

Religious scriptures have been venerated as the storehouse of higher knowledge of the essence of life. Be it any scripture – the Bhagavad Gita, the Bible, the Quran, Kabbalistic scriptures, the Upanishads, the Guru Granth Sahib, Buddhist scriptures on the Dhamma, the Dasbodh, the Dnyaneshwari, or transcribed conversations with Self-realized masters – every attempt has been made to transcribe, safeguard and pass them across generations.

Half-secret
> Acquire wisdom by reading and analyzing religious scriptures to attain God.

The recital of scriptures has been followed as a custom in various cultures. While it is possible that such recitals could become mechanical and ritualistic, those who thirst for knowledge can find such recitals interesting and intellectually rewarding.

Scriptures are the compositions of knowledge. However, there is a difference between knowledge and knowing. Knowledge is stored and recalled from memory. Knowing is the ongoing experience of awareness. Knowledge is done and dusted. Knowing is alive and fresh.

Truth is subjective experience, not objective knowledge. It cannot be known as you would know the other topics of the world. You can only experience it by 'being' it. And to 'be' it, you need to empty yourself of all that you have learned about the Truth. You need to release all the beliefs that you have gathered this far. This requires true faith and devotion, which can be awakened in the presence of a true Guru.

You cannot borrow the Truth from outside; it cannot be obtained. This is because it is already available within you. The best scripture to study to experience the truth is your own Self. When a true master points at the truth within you, it is by this grace that true wisdom awakens within you.

The Risk of Being Misguided

The scriptures have been venerated as the Truth. They speak about the Truth; they can point to the Truth. The Truth expressed in the scriptures arose from the experience that Self-realized masters reveled in. They are a reflection of the direct experience of the Truth. They serve as a mirror. But the mirror is not the Truth.

Moreover, the mirror is tainted with dust. The reflection of the Truth has been distorted through years of interpretation and commentaries, mostly by those who lacked the direct experience of the Self.

Consider the grand aphorism declared in the Upanishads: "Aham Brahmasmi". This declaration arose from the experience of the Self. This has been literally translated by many interpreters as "I am God", "I am that all-pervading reality".

However, such translations can cause the seeker to believe that he is the God personified. A person can never be God. The deeper import of the aphorism can be stated as, "God is the I-AM". This may sound grammatically incorrect. And yet, it means that God is the "I-AMness"; God is that sense of existence; God is the living presence within every body-mind. This is what Jesus meant when he declared, "I AM that I AM". Interpretations and translations that do not arise from the experience of the Self mislead the seeker away from the essence of the Truth.

When scriptures are transcribed, they are the expression of a realized master. The master bestows grace through the medium of words. But when one holds onto scriptures and invests in mere words and their empirical meanings, then one gets lost in the pointers and loses what they are pointing at.

When you enjoy a candy, you eat the candy and throw away the stick on which it was held. Words are like the stick. They are meant to convey the essence, which is beyond words. Once the essence is grasped, the role of words is over.

Commentaries and interpretations of the Truth lack the potency of a realized master's presence. The teachings and the instructions delivered by the living Guru have a very deep impact. If you try to hit someone with a bullet held in your hand, the bullet won't have an impact. But the Guru is like a gun. When the bullet is shot from the gun it hits the person with tremendous momentum and has a grave impact on him.

In the same way, if the disciple listens to the Truth from someone else, then the impact is like the bullet thrown from the hand. When the disciple listens to the same words, the same knowledge, from the living Guru, his ego is eliminated. This is because the words delivered by the living Guru come directly from the experience of the Self. They arise from the quintessence of Truth.

Hurdles with Self-Study and Analysis of Scriptures

Suppose the eyeglasses were to say that they want to see the eyes, what would you tell them? You would tell them, "You cannot see. You are only a medium through which the eyes see the world." The glasses cannot see the eye. It is the eye that sees through the glasses. In the same way, the human body-mind can never know the Self. It is the Self that experiences and expresses itself through the human body-mind.

Gathering knowledge to grasp the Truth is like the glasses that wish to see the eye! You can continue to stuff the mind with conceptual knowledge, ornate with logical reasoning, but all this has nothing to do with the true Self. The mind imagines the Self in terms of concepts and prejudices that have been imprinted in memory. Concepts create barriers. To be able to experience the immaculate Self, one needs to unlearn what one has held as knowledge.

Full-secret

> Empty yourself, get rid of past conditioning, and transcend what is known. Abide in non-dual trans-ignorance – your true nature.

It is only with true faith and devotion that one can let go of such bookish knowledge and abide in the pure Truth. It is then that true realization of the depth and grandeur of the Truth becomes evident. Else, one loses it in intellectual delights of knowledge that is available in poetic lines, scriptural verses and hearsay. Such knowledge does not serve the real purpose.

The ego needs to realize that it is a hurdle in the experience of the Truth. Someone, who has been searching for God in the temple, says, "Where is God? I've searched him all around here. I can't find him." He will be told, "God is standing right behind you, but is hidden because you are standing tall. You only need to bend low and bow down, and He will be revealed."

The highest use of the intellect is in realizing its own limitations. The highest use of reasoning is in realizing the limited confines of logic when it comes to experiencing the Truth.

The intellect should be trained for subtler contemplation to a point where it realizes the futility of stuffing knowledge and holding onto concepts. True wisdom lies in becoming empty. Become an empty flute through which divine music can flow.

Expression of the Truth That is Beyond Words

The whole world of forms and phenomena is the expression of the Truth, the Self. It can be said that all that exists is the Truth, God, Consciousness – whatever you like to call it. But the mind cannot grasp this. When you seek God in terms of what you already know, it poses a hurdle in experiencing what is so obvious.

True Wisdom is experiential. True Wisdom can be called 'Knowlerience'. This is a new word that is needed to explain this. Prevalent words like "knowledge" and "experience" instantly bring up preconceived notions that are held within you. A new vocabulary is required to transcend these notions and interpreted meanings.

'Knowlerience' is the realization of the Truth through non-conceptual experience. Non-conceptual, because, it cannot be grasped through concepts, it cannot be known through thinking, it cannot be deduced through reasoning.

The Self cannot be explained in words, but it can be pointed at. However, there is a risk that the seeker of Truth may get caught up with the pointers and completely miss what they are pointing at.

> A young child once asked his father what the color green looked like. The father, whose finger was stained with red ink, pointed the stained finger in the direction of a tree and said, "That's

green." The child, instead of looking at the tree beyond the two of them, fixed his gaze on his father's stained finger and said, "Yes. I understand."

You can see that he has mistaken the red stain on his father's finger to be green. The child then carries this misunderstanding with him throughout his life after mistaking the color of the pointing finger to be the color of what was being pointed at.

In the same way, people may spend their lifetime imprisoned in the limitations of thoughts and yet, they may claim to have experienced the Self. But, like the young child in this example, they really do not truly know it through direct experience.

One may say, "I can feel the presence of the Self." Another may say, "The experience of the Self is blissful." and yet another may say, "The Self cannot be described." These statements have nothing to do with the real experience of the Self. These are mere qualifying statements that arise as thoughts – and thoughts can never define the Self. The most we can do is to point to the Self.

The Self has been pointed at in various ways. Many who have realized the Self have written, spoken, and sung about it. But all these forms of expression are merely pointers, nothing more than stained fingers!

Many seekers spend their lives paying attention to the pointers instead of to what they are pointing. They argue about them all through their lives; they never look beyond these pointers.

Pointers belong in the realm of thoughts. The Self is from where thoughts originate. Thinking about the experience of the Self has nothing to do with actually experiencing the Self. When you look past these pointers and experience consciousness, you experience freedom from the shackles of concepts.

With anything that you absorb from the world, you fill your mind. You stuff yourself with input that does not serve the real purpose. For example, whatever you hear on the TV or the radio, be it entertainment or information from the Discovery channel will fill you up. They will unconsciously cause impressions in your subconscious mind. You become fixated with these impressions.

Words arising from Truth serve you by emptying your mind. They bring about an un-conditioning of the mind. They break your attachment to the body-mind, so that you can see everything as-it-is.

Attaining the State Beyond Knowledge

When they are told that the experience of the Self is beyond knowledge, the quick question that is raised is, "How can we experience the state beyond knowledge?"

The question to be asked is: Who is aspiring to attain that state beyond knowledge? Who is trying to grasp the experience of Self? Is the mind going to experience it? No.

The mind desires to be present and know the experience of the Self. It is only when the judging and aspiring mind drops, that the Self can experience itself. You need to reach the state of trans-ignorance. Trans-ignorance is not the ignorance of the mind. It is the openness of the mind to whatever is. The mind no longer holds fixations or makes stories out of what is being experienced. One transcends both knowledge and ignorance and begins to experience life just like a child. One rests in the peace of 'not knowing' and allows life to unfold in a state of wonder.

When you stop labeling whatever is being experienced in terms of what is already known, every experience becomes fresh, as if it's the first time. The world, that was appearing dead and dull due to the curtain of labels, begins to appear lively and vibrant. The light of awareness shines in everything that is being known.

This light of awareness cannot be found in books. It can only be experienced within yourself in pure silence, beyond noise and quietude, beyond thoughts, beyond everything that is known. It is the light of knowing, of awareness in which you perceive not only light, but also darkness.

When people do not recognize this light of knowing, which is constantly illumining their lives, they tend to be lost in whatever is being known. Whatever is being known has nothing to do with the experience of the ultimate knower.

You allow the experience of the Self by immersing yourself in the love of the Self, by surrendering yourself to divine will. It is only when the individual personality vanishes through understanding that the Self reveals itself to itself.

Return to the innocence of a child, where you live in the wonder of 'not-knowing' and allow life to unfold. With this alone can you break free from the prison, bound by beliefs and philosophies.

The Truth is the Open Secret

The Truth is an open secret. It is so obvious that one easily misses it.

Suppose you are searching for a bar of chocolate in a house. You search everywhere, in the drawing room, in the kitchen, in the bedrooms; you search every nook-and-corner; you go through each and every drawer and closet, but are unable to find it.

How would you feel like if you were then told that the entire house, its walls, furniture, everything… is made of chocolate!

All the time, you were in frenzy, searching the chocolate in a particular wrapper… and so, you were missing what was obvious all the time.

In the same way, the all-pervading consciousness is enlivening every aspect of our life. It is the underlying essence of every moment that we are alive. Yet, we easily miss it, because we seek it in the wrappers of concepts and ideologies.

There is one sentence to be remembered and repeat in every life situation: "All I know is that I don't know." Be open and receive life as it unfolds.

20

The Twofold Path Leading to One

Seekers of Truth tread various paths in their journey towards Self-realization. Some of the established and well-known approaches to spiritual pursuit are *Gyan* (path of wisdom), *Dhyan* (path of meditation), *Karma* (path of conscious action), *Japa* (path of chanting), and *Bhakti* (path of devotion).

> ### Half-secret
> Karma-yoga, Bhakti-yoga, and Gyan-yoga are distinct paths that lead the seeker to Self-realization.

All these paths are essentially meant to defocus the attention and energies of the seeker from worldly aspects and direct them within on the Self. The mind undergoes a transformation and reaches a state of quietism, where it mentally withdraws from worldly interests and revels in the divine presence of the Self within.

This is symbolized in Hindu mythology by Nandi, the bull that serves as Lord Shiva's escort. Nandi is depicted in a sitting posture, facing the sanctum of the Lord. The white color symbolizes purity of mind. Also, the bull sits bowing towards the sanctum of Lord Shiva. This symbolizes an attunement to the divine principle within. It is as if Nandi is seated in a meditative state of waiting.

Vital Qualities Leading to Self-Attunement

On the journey to Self-realization, the seeker develops certain vital qualities that are essential to abide in Self-experience. Following are the key qualities that are developed in the journey.

- *Viveka* is the ability to discriminate between the real and the unreal, between the permanent and the non-permanent.

- *Vairagya* is the dispassion for the enjoyment of worldly objects. It is a withdrawal from sensory indulgence. True and lasting dispassion is born from *Viveka*. It comes when one is rooted in the conviction of the futility and impermanence of worldly pursuits. Dispassion, that comes due to loss of property or loss in the family cannot last for long.

- *Titiksha* is the capacity of forbearance, the ability to endure the pairs of opposites like heat and cold, pleasure and pain, praise and criticism, happiness and sorrow, etc.

- *Sama* and *Dama* bring the state of withdrawal of the senses from sensory indulgences. The senses are directed inward, as depicted by Nandi.

- *Uparati* is the state of quietism and equipoise, which is very essential to abide in the stillness of Self-experience.
- *Mumukshatva* is the intense yearning for liberation. This yearning is not lukewarm; it is boiling. Such yearning can catapult the mind to surrender totally to the divine will.

Seekers belonging to various lineages of saints, tend to follow the specific prescribed paths to attain these qualities. Those who follow the path of wisdom, stress on developing a strong intellect that can understand the subtle aspects of the truth. They seek to understand the absolute nature of reality. Those who follow the path of devotion, revel in divine surrender. They live in a state of surrender, worship and sing praises of the Lord.

However, the contrasting approaches of these paths have led to them being fitted into separate silos. Those who seek wisdom do not agree with the approach of devotion… and vice-versa.

The full-secret unravels the integrity of all the paths that lead to the Truth. It expounds the missing link in understanding these seemingly contrasting approaches. When the missing link is grasped, these paths begin to appear as aspects of an integrated approach.

THE INTEGRATION OF THE PATHS TO THE TRUTH

All the prevalent paths that lead to the attainment of Truth can broadly be divided into just two – the Path of Wisdom and the Path of Devotion.

The Path of Devotion is the path of surrender to the divine will of God. It is the path of submitting to Consciousness–the Source of everything. Effort in this path is effortless, as actions happen in joyous surrender to the Self.

The Path of Wisdom is that of will power, where the seeker of Truth applies his intellect to grasp the Truth and internalize it.

The Path of Devotion is akin to a kitten, which leaves its body loose and gives itself up to its mother, who then carries it around with her mouth. The Path of Wisdom is like that of a baby monkey that needs to clasp onto its mother's belly when she jumps from one branch to the other. The kitten surrenders. The baby monkey clutches with all its might.

All the paths that are known in spirituality finally culminate in this two-fold path. It is one and the same path with two aspects – the aspect of complete surrender and the aspect of reasoning and meditation. The seeker of Self-realization needs guidance on both these paths.

Devotion and Wisdom Complement Each Other

> There were two travelers who needed to cross safely through a jungle to return home. One of them was blind, while the other did not have legs. Individually, they could not have made it home. The lame traveler climbed onto the shoulders of his blind companion and started guiding him through the jungle. The blind man followed his directions and walked carefully, carrying him through the perils of the jungle. Both managed to reach home safely.

So it is on the path of Self-realization. The lame man symbolizes the eye of wisdom, while the blind one represents the legs of devotion. Without the legs of devotion, the eyes of wisdom cannot walk the path. And the legs of devotion cannot see the path without the eyes of wisdom. Let devotion obtain the eyes of wisdom and let wisdom in turn receive the legs of devotion.

The seeker who pursues the path of wisdom through the practice of meditation and conscious actions develops unswerving faith, thereby leading to the surrender of his individual personhood to the Self. The one who follows the path of devotion matures in understanding of the Truth.

Finally, the one who works on gaining wisdom surrenders and the one who surrenders attains wisdom. Thus, both the paths merge at its culmination in Self-realization.

Tejgyan is the understanding that integrates these paths - those on the path of wisdom attain devotion and those on the path of devotion attain wisdom. You begin directly with the understanding that brings together both Wisdom and Devotion.

You do not have to decide which path is best for you. Whatever the mind prefers need not be the best path for you. Following the path that the mind feels like is like asking a thief how he would like to be captured. The thief would never give away the path that would lead to his downfall. Similarly, the aspect of the mind that considers itself as a separate individual has to drop. That aspect of the mind cannot be trusted to decide which path to tread. Leave how this happens to grace. Ultimately, grace is the only way.

Karma and Meditation Complement Each Other

Both, Karma-yoga (the path of right action) and Dhyana-yoga (the path of meditation) are essentially the practice of wisdom.

Karma-yoga is not actually a path. It is the practice of conscious action backed by higher understanding. It is wisdom-in-action. The seeker applies effort to transmute higher understanding into action.

Any occupation that you choose is merely a field of activity that serves the higher purpose of Self-realization and Self-expression. Functioning in your chosen field of activity serves you to discover your true nature, build conviction in it and to be established in the experience of your true nature. Conscious action in all facets of your life propels you towards this ultimate aim behind all the aims that you pursue.

The practice of conscious action slowly shifts the earnest seeker from doing into being. With consistent practice of conscious action, one begins to increasingly abide in Self-awareness. In this state of detached being, one goes beyond doing and non-doing. One simply witnesses actions arising as the spontaneous play of happening. Through the practice of abiding in this state, the notion of separateness dissolves and actions become a cause for liberation.

The practice of meditation has been grossly misunderstood as that of inaction. This is a missing link. Meditation is the state of being absorbed in the Self. Meditation is your essential nature. When viewed as the state of being in Self-awareness, meditation has nothing to do with doing or non-doing. It is not an escape from the world. One can be engaged in action while being absorbed in the state of Self-meditation.

The term, Meditation, is also used to refer to the practice that leads to this state. Meditation, when viewed as this practice, is a way of stilling the mind. The mind tends to indulge in thoughts of the world. Incessant thinking becomes a habit. It is a compulsive dis-ease, as it keeps you away from the state of complete ease. The practice of meditation helps you detach from thoughts that plague your awareness. It raises awareness of pure consciousness.

The daily practice of meditation is a preparation to connect with the world in the right way. It prepares you to abide in awareness of Self, while being engaged in worldly activity.

Just as the paths of wisdom and devotion are complementary, one naturally leading to the other, similarly the practice of meditation and right karma are complementary too. One naturally leads to the other.

The more you dwell in the state of meditation on Self, it serves as a thinner that weakens your attachment to the mind's notions, beliefs, and tendencies. The habit of identifying with personality is weakened. You remain absorbed in pure consciousness – the very light in which everything appears.

Being absorbed in the Self automatically transforms your action. Your actions become increasingly non-personalized, arising from the immaculate standpoint of totality. Actions happen not from the notion of 'doing', but from the essence of 'being'. In this way, meditation translates into inspired action.

The converse is also true. The practice of conscious action backed by higher understanding naturally leads the seeker into a meditative state. When actions are performed in the remembrance of the Self, one rises beyond doing and non-doing. Detached witnessing gains precedence. While actions happen through the body-mind, the detached witnessing presence becomes increasingly prominent. Every action is an opportunity, an invitation to honor the divine presence that enlivens it.

Meditation is like downloading a media file in offline mode for later viewing. Meditation is practiced by being in the stillness of presence. You cleanse your past conditioning by allowing it to rise into your awareness and watching it as a detached witness.

The practice of conscious karma is like online streaming video. You watch the video in real-time as it is being downloaded. In the same way, the practice of conscious karma happens in and through your daily interactions in the world. You cleanse your mind of past conditioning by encountering it through your interactions with the world. Every situation, every incident serves as an opportunity to practice conscious karma.

Thus, the one who delves into the depth of Self-meditation naturally begins to manifest inspired actions arising from the non-personal standpoint of the Self. And the one who acts by abiding in constant remembrance of the Self naturally begins to settle into the stillness of Self-meditation.

Full-secret

> Performing conscious karma in the spirit of wisdom is true devotion. Karma, Devotion and Wisdom are aspects of one and the same thing. Ultimately there are only two paths — the path of wisdom and the path of devotion. Both lead to one another.

Since both meditation and karma are aspects of the Path of Wisdom, both ways, finally culminate in devotion.

THE CONGRUENCE OF KARMA, WISDOM AND DEVOTION

Ultimately, karma, devotion, and wisdom converge in the one experience of the Self.

Performing conscious karma in the spirit of wisdom is true devotion.

Performing awakened action in the light of recognition of the Self is devotion. This statement unites the three approaches into one. We find that karma, wisdom and devotion are aspects of one and the same thing.

However, mere intellectual understanding of this does not suffice. We may know about the Truth; but we need to live by it. This understanding should permeate all action. This is where devotion plays an important role.

There are many intellectual seekers who believe that an intellectual understanding of the Truth is enough. They believe that devotion is not their cup of tea. They need to realize that wisdom can function only through the medium of devotion.

There are people who flaunt their knowledge and indulge in intellectual discussions. The only result is intellectual entertainment. It does not serve to drop their ego.

There is a risk, inherent with acquiring knowledge. Knowledge is mere information. It can make one egotistic and arrogant. When one believes that one knows, one shuts his ears to further learning.

True wisdom is beyond knowledge. True wisdom comes with devotion, with the attitude of surrender to life. It comes with unconditional acceptance to the way life unfolds.

■ ■ ■

You can mail your opinion or feedback on this book to:
books.feedback@tejgyan.org

Bibliography

For further reading on the topics discussed in this book, please refer the following titles, authored by Sirshree.

Chapter No.	Chapter Name	Reference Title
1.	Bringing Completeness to Prayer	Excuse Me Dear God
2.	Beyond Virtuousness	Dip into Oneness
3.	True Love – the Wellspring Within You	Celebrating Relationships
5.	Dissolving Problems	The Little Gita of Problem Solving
6.	Beyond Personality and Character	Inner Ninety Hidden Infinity
7.	The Ultimate Goal of Life	Answers that Awaken
8.	You are Meditation	You are Meditation
10.	The Motivation for Karma	100% Karma
11.	The Basis for Result of Karma	100% Karma
12.	Whatever Happens is for Growth	The Source
13.	The Magic of Forgiveness	Seek Forgiveness and Be Free
17	Align with the Divine Will	Essence of Devotion
19.	Transcending Knowledge	100% Wisdom

About Sirshree

Sirshree's spiritual quest, which began during his childhood, led him on a journey through various schools of philosophy and meditation practices. He studied a wide range of literature on mind science and spirituality. After a long period of deep contemplation on the truth of life, his quest culminated in attaining the ultimate truth.

Sirshree espouses, "All spiritual paths that lead to the truth begin differently but culminate at the same point – Understanding. This understanding is complete in itself. Listening to this understanding is enough to attain the Truth." Over the last two decades, he has dedicated his life to raise mass consciousness.

Sirshree has delivered more than 4000 discourses that throw light on this understanding. He has designed a system for wisdom, which makes it accessible to all. This system has inspired people from all walks of life to progress on their journey of the Truth. Thousands of seekers join in a virtual prayer for World Peace and Global Healing daily at 9:09 am and 9:09 pm.

About Tej Gyan Foundation

Tej Gyan Foundation is a non-profit organization founded on the teachings of Sirshree. The Foundation disseminates Tejgyan – the wisdom that guides one from self-development to Self-realization, leading towards Self-stabilization.

The Foundation's system for imparting wisdom has been assessed by international quality auditors and accredited with the ISO 9001:2015 certification. This wisdom has been presented in a simple, systematic, and practically applicable form that makes it accessible to people from all walks of life, regardless of religion, caste, social strata, country, or belief system.

The Foundation has centers in more than 400 cities and towns across India and other countries. The mission of Tej Gyan Foundation is to create a highly evolved society by leading seekers from negative thoughts to positive thoughts and further, from positive thoughts to Happy thoughts. A 'Happy thought' is the auspicious thought of being free from all thoughts, leading to the state of supreme bliss beyond thoughts.

If you seek such wisdom that leads you beyond mere knowledge, dissolves all problems, frees you from all limiting beliefs, reveals the true nature of divinity, and establishes you in the ultimate truth, then it is time to discover Tejgyan; it is time to rise above the mundane knowledge of words and experience Tejgyan!

The MahaAasmani Magic of Awakening Retreat

Self-development to Self-realization towards Self-stabilization

Do you wish to experience unconditional happiness that is not dependent on any reason? Happiness that is permanent and only increases with time? Do you wish to experience love, peace, self-belief, harmony in relationships, prosperity, and true contentment? Do you wish to progress in all facets of your life, viz. physical, mental, social, financial, and spiritual?

If you seek answers to these questions and are thirsty for the ultimate truth, then you are welcome to participate in the MahaAasmani Magic of Awakening retreat organized by Tej Gyan Foundation. This is the Foundation's flagship retreat based on the teachings of Sirshree.

The purpose of this retreat

The purpose of this retreat is that every human being should:

- Discover the answer to "Who am I" and "Why am I?" through direct experience and be established in ultimate bliss.

- Learn the art of living in the present, free from the burden of the past and the anxiety of the future.

- Acquire practical tools to help quieten the chattering mind and dissolve problems.

- Discover missing links in the practices of Meditation (*Dhyana*), Action (*Karma*), Wisdom (*Gyana*), and Devotion (*Bhakti*).

About Books by Sirshree

Sirshree's published work includes more than 150 book titles, some of which have been translated into more than 10 languages. His literature provides a profound reading on various topics of practical living and unravels the missing links in karma, wisdom, devotion, meditation, and consciousness.

His books have been published by leading publishing houses like Penguin, Hay House, Bloomsbury, Wisdom Tree, Jaico, etc. "The Source" book series, authored by Sirshree, has sold over 10 million copies. Various luminaries and celebrities like His Holiness the Dalai Lama, publishers Mr. Reid Tracy, Ms. Tami Simon and Yoga Master Dr. B. K. S. Iyengar have released Sirshree's books and lauded his work.

The Source
Attain Both, Inner Peace
and Worldly success

Awaken the Power of Faith
Discover the 7 Principles of the
Highest Power of the Universe

To order books authored by Sirshree, login to:
www.gethappythoughts.org
For further details, call: +91 9011013210

Tej Gyan Foundation – Contact details

Registered Office:
Happy Thoughts Building, Vikrant Complex, Near Tapovan Mandir,
Pimpri, Pune 411017, INDIA. Contact: +91 20-27411240, +91 20-27412576

MaNaN Ashram:
Survey No. 43, Sanas Nagar, Nandoshi Gaon, Kirkatwadi Phata,
Off Sinhagad Road, Taluka Haveli, Pune district - 411024, INDIA.
Contact: +91 992100 8060.

WORLD PEACE PRAYER

Divine Light of Love, Bliss, and Peace is Showering;

The Golden Light of Higher Consciousness is Rising;

All negativity on Earth is Dissolving;

Everyone is in Peace and Blissfully Shining;

O God, Gratitude for Everything!

Members of Tej Gyan Foundation have been offering this impersonal mass prayer for many years. Those who are happy can offer this prayer. Those feeling low or suffering from illness can receive healing with this prayer.

If you are feeling troubled or sick, please sit to receive the healing effect of this prayer. Visualize that the divine white healing light is being showered on earth through the prayers of thousands and is also reaching you, bringing you peace and good health. You can dwell in this feeling for some time and then offer your gratitude to those offering the prayer.

A Humble Appeal

More than a million peace lovers pray for World Peace and Global Healing every morning and evening at 9:09. Also, a prayer (in Hindi) to elevate consciousness is webcast every day on YouTube at 3:30 pm and 9:00 pm IST. Please participate in this noble endeavor.

www.ingramcontent.com/pod-product-compliance
Lightning Source LLC
LaVergne TN
LVHW040142080526
838202LV00042B/2992